TWAYNE'S WORLD AUTHORS SERIES

A Survey of the World's Literature

Sylvia E. Bowman, Indiana University

GENERAL EDITOR

NEW ZEALAND

Joseph Jones, University of Texas

EDITOR

William Satchell

(TWAS 35)

TWAYNE'S WORLD AUTHORS SERIES (TWAS)

*The purpose of TWAS is to survey the major writers
—novelists, dramatists, historians, poets, philosophers,
and critics—of the nations of the world. Among the
national literatures covered are those of Australia,
Canada, China, Eastern Europe, France, Germany,
Greece, India, Italy, Japan, Latin America, New Zealand, Poland, Russia, Scandinavia, Spain, and the
African nations, as well as Hebrew, Yiddish, and
Latin Classical literatures. This survey is comple-
mented by Twayne's United States Authors Series
and English Authors Series*

*The intent of each volume in these series is to present
a critical-analytical study of the works of the writer;
to include biographical and historical material that
may be necessary for understanding, appreciation,
and critical appraisal of the writer; and to present all
material in clear, concise English—but not to vitiate
the scholarly content of the work by doing so.*

William Satchell

By PHILLIP *John* WILSON

Twayne Publishers, Inc.   ::   New York

Books by Phillip Wilson

The Outcasts
Pacific Flight
Beneath the Thunder
The Maorilander
Some Are Lucky

Foreword

AN EFFLORESCENCE of talent such as New Zealand has shown for the past decade, and more, inevitably invokes inquiry into origins. As a practising novelist of the younger school, Mr. Wilson not only acknowledges his own debt to William Satchell but provides a means of access to the work of the one early New Zealand novelist who most clearly deserves the name of pioneer. The reader of this study will come to see how Satchell discovered for himself, and helped others discover, what it meant to adapt one's literary tastes and talents (not always with perfect success) to a new land. Such a transposition, in the words of the Auckland poet Allen Curnow, "... was something different, something / Nobody counted on."

Preface

WILLIAM SATCHELL is the most powerful early New Zealand novelist. Few men have endured such neglect as attended the publication of his novel *The Greenstone Door* in 1914—only to have the enthusiastic revival of it occur twenty-one years later. He was the first writer to speak eloquently for brown New Zealand. His novels burn with a fiery anger against the contemptuous attitude of many nineteenth-century settlers toward the Maoris.

These pages are a revision of my earlier essay on William Satchell, entitled *The Maorilander*. But if the writing of them was principally an act of homage to the pioneer who has been my inspiration and true master novelist beyond any other, they are also a criticism—of his work as a painter of early New Zealand society, especially with regard to his romanticism; of his obsession with the conflict between civilization and the wilderness; of his doubts about progress and about Christianity.

Satchell was an Englishman who emigrated to New Zealand in 1886, when he was twenty-six. A great deal of his early life in London remains a mystery, and we are left with the riddle of his novels and short stories written in New Zealand. His novels reveal the working of a mind of exceptional power. In the division of the literary and intellectual world of his time between the followers of Yeats and the followers of Shaw, he fell inevitably on the side of the poet and visionary, rather than on that of the socialist and naturalist.

When he worked in London as a poet and publisher before his emigration, the woman he loved, two volumes of whose poetry he published, and whose poem "A Little Bird" he preserved all his life in her neat handwriting on a scrap of paper, was May Probyn, who is remembered now as a friend of Yeats. Yeats was five years younger than Satchell and he returned to London to begin work as a poet the year after Satchell left for New Zealand. Yet Satchell wrote poetic dramas as Yeats did; he read deeply during his formative years in German Romanticism as Yeats did so that it became an important and long-lasting force in his life. He rejected the mechanism of modern science as Yeats did. *The Celtic Twilight* came out in the same year that he wrote his own drama, *Hemeroma*, in which, if the unpublished manuscript still exists, I think we would find many of the speeches, confrontations, and ideas incorporated in *The Greenstone Door.*

Some of Satchell's works do survive in manuscript. These include *The Fall of the House Linoha* (undated), *Plays and Poems 1882-83, Poems and Tales* (undated), *The Nihilist: A Metrical Tragedy in Four Acts* (1893), and *The Book of Joso* (1928). I have not attempted to read this unpublished material so I cannot assess its value, though I don't believe it is very great. Nor have I been able to locate "The Other Inmate," which may be a poem, a play, or a short story published in some newspaper; or the script of "an unpublished novel which is a story of racing in New Zealand early days" referred to by Eric G. Cowell in a letter dated March 9, 1942, in the Satchell Papers in the Alexander Turnbull Library. Cowell also mentions "one serial story in a southern daily," but this could be "The Stone Stable Mystery" in the *Graphic.* One further point that Cowell mentions is that "a breakdown in the young author's health caused him to leave England." Is this true?

In addition to his novels I have read the short stories he published, often anonymously or over a nom-de-plume, in early New Zealand magazines and newspapers. Some of this work remains inaccessible and there may be more of his stories in the old files. But besides the material I used for *The Maorilander,* I have located two important new short stories.

I gratefully acknowledge the information given me by George Satchell, and his permission to quote from his father's novels, stories, and poems. Acknowledgements are also made to the following publishers for permission to quote from the novels to which they hold copyright: Methuen and Co. for *The Land of the Lost;* Macmillan and Co. for *The Toll of the Bush;* Chapman and Hall for *The Elixir of Life;* Sidgwick and Jackson for *The Greenstone Door;* also to Whitcombe and Tombs for permission to use material from *The Maorilander.* Finally I am very glad to have been able to consult the unpublished Doctoral thesis of an American student, Miss Nancy Wall, on Maori themes in New Zealand fiction, which was written recently while she was a Fulbright Scholar in this country.

P. W.

Wellington,
New Zealand.

Contents

Chronology

1860   William Arthur Satchell, elder son of Thomas Satchell and Hannah Mordey Satchell, born on February 1st at Gray's Inn, London, England.

ca. 1866–
1876   Educated at Grove House Academy and Hurstpierpoint College.

ca. 1877–
1878   Studied at Heidelberg University.

1879   Returned to London. Managed publishing house of Satchell, Peyton and Co., later called W. Satchell and Co.

1883   *Bedlam Ballads and Straitwaistcoat Stories* published in February; *Will O' The Wisp and Other Tales in Prose and Verse* published in October.

1884   Collapse of publishing business.

1885   Continued writing poetry at Downshire Hill House, Hampstead.

1886   Left London for New Zealand on May 21st. Settled at Waima in Hokianga County on a 400-acre block of Maori land. Worked on the land for five years as a pioneer settler.

1889   Married Susan Bryers, daughter of George Bryers, settler, and Mary Bryers (formerly Herau) in Hokianga on November 15th.

1890   Daughter Edith Hannah born at Waima.

1891   Gave up land lease and worked as storekeeper at Rawene; considered petitioning Parliament over loss of his land, because the Maori title deed was invalid.

1892   Moved to Auckland. Son Thomas Arthur born in Parnell, Auckland.

1893   Susan and the children returned to the Hokianga to live with her aunt in April because of financial difficulties. William remained in Auckland. Son Allan born at Rawene. The *Nihilist, A Metrical Tragedy in Four Acts, The Cadet,* a novel, "Hinemoa," a long poem, and *Hemeroma,* a poetic drama, written but not published.

1894   "Rondeau" (March 10th) and "The Great Unemployed Scheme" (June 16th) published in *The New Zealand Graphic,* followed by other poems and stories up to January, 1896. Susan returned to Auckland.

1895   Son William Mordey born in Ponsonby, Auckland.

1895–   Made money during the second Thames-Coromandel
1899   gold boom by working as sharebroker.

1897   Daughter Alice Elane born at Ponsonby, Auckland.

1900   Moved to Grange Road, Mount Roskill, Auckland. *Patriotic and Other Poems* published.

1901   *The Maorilander,* a weekly magazine, published February 8th-March 22nd. Daughter Mary Victoria born at Mount Roskill.

1902   *The Land of the Lost* published. "The Ballad of Stuttering Jim" included in *The Bulletin Reciter.*

1903   Son Hugh Hurst born at Mount Roskill.

1905   *The Toll of the Bush* published. Son George Francis born at Mount Roskill.

1906   Moved to Hauraki Street, Birkenhead. Further financial troubles.

1907   *The Elixir of Life* published.

1909   Became secretary of the Auckland Horticultural Society. Play, *The Divided Note,* completed but not produced.

1910   Moved to Church Street, Northcote. Began work on *The Greenstone Door.*

1911   Daughter Rosalind born at Northcote. Moved to Onewa Road, Birkenhead, with five-acre orchard and poultry farm.

1912–   Took part in the Auckland Exhibition as horticulturist.
1913

1914   *The Greenstone Door* published.

1915–   Wrote numerous articles on war for *The New Zealand*

1918   *Herald's* Saturday Supplement. Sons Thomas, William, and Allan fighting in France and Palestine.

1917– Worked for Stanley P. Gibbons Timber Company at
1928   Kopu, Thames, as accountant.

1919   Gave up secretaryship of Auckland Horticultural Society.

1928   Returned to Auckland to live at Malvern Road, Morningside. Continued to work for Gibbons company. *The Book of Joso* written but not published.

1932   Moved to 37 Queensway, Mount Roskill, Auckland.

1935   *The Greenstone Door* reprinted.

1936   Stanley P. Gibbons Timber Company went out of business.

1937   Susan Satchell died in Auckland.

1938   *The Land of the Lost* reprinted.

1939   Awarded Civil List Pension by the New Zealand Government in recognition of his work as a novelist.

1942   William Satchell died on October 21st in Auckland.

CHAPTER 1

Poet into Pioneer

IN the year 1902 a new novelist emerged in world literature. He came from two small, remote islands in the South Pacific Ocean, where the first organized settlement from Europe had begun little more than sixty years previously. The novelist was William Satchell, who had emigrated to New Zealand in 1886 from London, England.

The novels of William Satchell are a product of that long colonizing movement of the English-speaking peoples, which reached into the Pacific after Captain James Cook's great voyages of exploration from 1769 to 1779. In New Zealand in particular, adventurers and settlers from Great Britain tried to create a kind of Utopia based on the best in Western civilization.

These frontier lands of early New Zealand are the milieu of Satchell's novels. As an artist and thinker he belongs to the nineteenth century romantic tradition: his fiction exalts the ideal of natural man and explores the idea of nature which had grown out of the American and French revolutions. Rousseau and Jefferson and Wordsworth were the origins of much of his thought, and the myths of the noble savage and the democratic, hard-working pioneer burn brightly for him.

After his arrival, William Satchell lived at the birthplace of New Zealand civilization as we now know it—the estuary of the Hokianga river, on the west coast of the North Auckland peninsula, where New Zealand's famous Polynesian discoverer, the Maori navigator Kupe (Koopay), first landed. This district forms the setting of his two early novels, *The Land of the Lost* and *The Toll of the Bush*.

With these books and his later work, Satchell greatly extended the range and depth of new Pacific fiction. In the days when the country was still a British colony—yet a time when New

Zealanders were already becoming conscious of themselves as a separate nation—he wrote his novels, short stories, and poems out of the struggles of pioneers who were men and women mainly of British birth as he himself was. He created a fictional world, illuminated by his personal vision of life and filled with varied portraits of nineteenth century man. He wrote at first about life on the kauri gum diggings and on the North Auckland river and bush settlements, but concentrated at last on the historic conflict between white settlers and Maoris, which led to the Taranaki and Waikato Wars of the 1860s. He ranged over pioneer New Zealand society from wealthy businesmen to bush farmers, from the Governor in his mansion to the shanties and palm huts of poor folk and social outcasts. He depicted all kinds of Maori people, and showed in his novels, through the desires, thoughts, dreams, and actions of New Zealanders of his day, universal patterns of behavior and high moral truths.

Satchell was one of those novelists of splendid humanity, whose imagination casts a glow of great compassion on the characters of his novels. He is witty and gay; and although misery and wickedness and evil do enter into his scheme of things, evil is not consistently triumphant. A large mind and broad tolerance produce the deep moral interest of his novels. His view of life is rounded and whole, yet as a writer he was continually concerned with the picturesque side of life—he introduced much local color into his books. He understood the dominating influence of nature in the world of the pioneers, but was mainly interested in individuals who repudiated society, and he questioned accepted social institutions and conventions.

The important phase of Satchell's literary life was the twenty-year period between 1894 and 1914, when he produced four novels, nearly thirty short stories, and a small volume of poems. This is not a great production; the reason lies in the kind of life the author was obliged to live in early New Zealand, where he had to earn his living by time-consuming activities outside his art. To understand a talent properly, the circumstances that brought it to maturity must be considered, and there is much in the life of Satchell that was romantic and unusual, just as there was a great deal in it that was dull, domestic, and ordinary.

The material for a life of William Satchell is somewhat limited. For most of the fifty-six years after his emigration he lived unnoticed in an Auckland suburb. Outwardly he was a petit bourgeois, a father of nine children, an accountant, a share-broker, a secretary, a journalist. But if his life lacked drama in its later aspects, it had much excitement, disappointment, and adventure to begin with.

Satchell grew up in England during the great depression of the 1870s and '80s, and made his long voyage across the world to the South Pacific when he was twenty-six. From 1886 to 1893 he worked as a pioneer settler on a grant of Maori land, whose title later proved invalid, in one of the most romantic regions of New Zealand. Those seven years in Hokianga County provided him with many of the materials and themes for his fiction. When he left that district for Auckland city, he worked, after a period of acute poverty, as a sharebroker. He made a modest fortune in the Thames gold boom of 1895-1899, but lost it during the final boom of 1905-1907. However, the intervening years of stability were his most prolific time as a writer. Then after another interval he produced his fourth and finest novel, which was followed by twenty-eight years of almost unbroken silence.

He saw a new society being created around him, and as a "small capitalist" and father of nine children he contributed materially to that creation. But his main contribution to New Zealand civilization was his art as a novelist. Modern critics like E. H. McCormick in his *New Zealand Literature: A Survey* (1959) see him as the most important novelist before 1914—an opinion with which Joan Stevens concurs in her *The New Zealand Novel 1860-1965* (1066). He was the most powerful and most talented writer of his era, yet his work was almost forgotten until it began to be reprinted in 1935. His contemporaries were mainly short story writers and comparatively unskilled novelists, so that today he stands out even more than he would otherwise have done, by the colonial sparseness of competition. It is only in the young Katherine Mansfield, in such a brilliant early story as "The Woman at the Store" (1912) that he has a worthy competitor; indeed the severe realism of this story is in marked contrast to his own romanticism. Nevertheless he was in his way a master of the craft of fiction, and *The Land of the Lost* and *The Toll of the Bush* are among the best examples of sustained craftsmanship in early New Zealand literature. His last, fiery novel, *The Greenstone Door,* transcends its romantic excesses by the skill of its narration as much as by the intensity of feeling behind its somber theme.

He had no great theory of the novel, except to say that "by avoiding harsh contrasts and incongruities, we can show life in its true proportions," as he wrote in 1907 to the English musician and composer, William Platt. But he learnt his task well. His mentors in the craft of fiction were British novelists like Dickens and Hardy and Stevenson, Americans like Mark Twain and Hawthorne, and Australians like Henry Lawson.

He was a slow, fastidious, unprolific writer. In general the language of his novels is elegant, formal, and at times archaic, like the language of the English world from which he had emigrated. But he made use of vernacular speech as he heard it on the Hokianga and in Auckland, and he polished the surface of his prose to produce a professional clarity and sparkle.

He had the advantage, for a New Zealand writer, to marry a woman of mixed British and Maori ancestry. His new allegiance revolutionized his thinking on racial problems. But while racial themes came to have an increasing importance in his work, his early experiences as a lonely immigrant—his feeling of being an exile on the New Zealand frontier of the 1890s—gave him an enormous compassion for all the downtrodden and outcast people of his world.

In his last novel he tried to speak for mankind as a whole, and to emphasize the multi-racial nature of man. It is this intensity of his idealism, which shines through his fictional world like a beautiful light, which combines with his profound romanticism to provide his novels with their distinctive tone and universal appeal.

1 *Will o' the Wisp*

According to his own account, William Satchell was born in Gray's Inn, London, England, on February 1, 1860. However, there is no registration of his birth, and no record of his baptism, nor is there any similar documentation of his parents' marriage. So there is some mystery about the exact circumstances of his origin, and he appears to have believed as a young man that he was an illegitimate child, in the sense that his parents were not legally married.

Nevertheless his father, Thomas Satchell, was a highly cultivated and respected senior British civil servant who lived with
his family of four children in the fashionable London suburb
of Hampstead. He was a scholar, a bibliographer, a student of
Egyptology, and a lexicographer, who had many friends among
writers, painters, and musicians. His daughter Rosemary ad-
mitted only two faults in him—his book-collecting mania and
his absorption in the publishing firm which eventually brought
financial disaster to the family. He became British Surveyor-
General before his sudden death in 1887 from stomach cancer.
According to Dr. John Rake, his grandson, he was a friend of
Tennyson, corresponded with Wilkie Collins, and was one of a
literary group which met regularly at the famous Fleet Street
restaurant, the Chesire Cheese. With Thomas Westwood he
made revised editions of Izaak Walton's *The Compleat Angler*
and of the *Bibliotheca Piscatoria*. He is also said to have helped
to preserve Keats's house in Keats Grove, near the old Satchell
home in Hampstead.

Of the children, William emigrated to New Zealand, Rosemary
married Dr. Hubert Rake of Shennington, Thomas visited New
Zealand and then went to live in Japan, where he married a
Japanese beauty, published translations of Japanese poetry,
edited for a while the *Japan Herald* in Yokohama, and taught
at the Middle School, Wakayama. The fourth child, Alice, was
apparently an early victim of poliomyelitis.

The family had a legendary connection with Dr. Henry
Sacheverell, an eighteenth century political demagogue. One
ancestor, John Satchell of Kettering, was the author, about the
year 1815, of *Thornton Abbey, or the Persecuted Daughter;
Moral, Interesting and Religious; in a Series of Letters; for the
Improvement of the Rising Generation,* with a Recommendatory
Preface by the late Rev. Andrew Fuller, secretary of the Baptist
Missionary Society. Another William Satchell published at
Loughborough in 1859 *The Duties of a Young Man: A Lecture,*
while Agnes F. Satchell published at Antigua in 1852 a volume
of *Miscellaneous Poems,* and at Loughborough in 1858, *Reminiscences of Missionary Life in the Caribbean Islands.* Kettering
and Loughborough are only twenty miles apart, and the latter
town was the home of Hannah Mordey, Satchell's mother.

Satchell remained in close touch with his mother's relatives.

Following his emigration he wrote to his cousin Margaret Mordey at regular intervals, and even promised to marry her when he returned to England after making his fortune in New Zealand. As events turned out he never returned. But some mystery does surround Satchell's mother, according to others in the family.

Little is known of Satchell's childhood. However, nis boyhood friend Allan Fea, who became an author, illustrator, and antiquarian, has written about him in his *Recollections of Sixty Years*. Fea describes their meeting at Grove House School in the Highgate Road, an old-fashioned Academy for Young Gentlemen whose headmaster was the Reverend Thomas Tough. Apparently Mr. Tough, rather like Dickens's Wackford Squeers, told all new boys he was going to grind it into them. His wrathful displays included hurling the most daring offenders among his pupils down the spiral stone staircase which led up to the big, bare schoolroom, warmed in winter with only one small coke fire. When any of the boarders at this private school had a cold he was fed with a liberal supply of Cayenne pepper through an improvised paper funnel, to cure him.

Fea gives an amusing account of the way the pupils got their revenge for this harsh treatment in the after-lunch Latin class, when the Reverend Mr. Tough was inclined to fall asleep. By slow and cautious degrees a pile of books would be built up on the corner of his desk, until it reached Tower of Babel proportions—whereupon any involuntary movement of the sleeping headmaster would send the books crashing down on his own head. Fea says it was William Satchell who usually erected these towers of books—"which devilry rather cemented our friendship than otherwise."

In one respect Satchell was better off than his school friend Fea: his father sent him to Hurstpierpoint College after he left Grove House School, and finally to Heidelberg University. Though he did not take a degree, he presumably received at Heidelberg the finish required of the well-educated young Englishman of his day. He must have been about nineteen when he returned from Germany wearing (again according to Allan Fea) "gorgeous side-whiskers, a velvet coat and smoking cap." But it was difficult for a young Englishman to get a job in those days of world-wide economic depression, even if he had been to Heidelberg.

Satchell's father set him up as manager of the family publishing business. His earliest venture as a publisher appears to have been *My Life as an Angler,* by William Henderson. The book was probably accepted by his father, but the imprint bears his own name: W. Satchell, Peyton and Co. It is dated 1879, and the address of the firm is given as 12 Tavistock Street, Covent Garden, London. This address was later changed to 19 Tavistock Street and finally after financial setbacks to Downshire Hill House, the Satchell family home. Peyton, who handled the printing side of the business, was the son of a friend of Satchell's father in the London Custom House where both parents were then working. Peyton soon dropped out and the firm became W. Satchell and Co.

As a publisher Satchell was a complete failure. The company was never registered, and it made no profits on its books, which included collections of folk tales, essays on aesthetics, and poetry. The most notable poems were by May Probyn, a friend of W. B. Yeats. Allan Fea remembers that Satchell imagined himself to be in love with May Probyn. He certainly preserved one of her manuscripts, "A Little Bird," all his life. The firm also put out two periodicals edited by Satchell's father: *The Anglers' Note-Book* and *The Tourist and Traveller.* Allan Fea and young Satchell contributed to the latter articles about walking tours they made together in search of old manor houses, crumbling and dilapidated castles, or baronial halls. One summer they made a pilgrimage on foot through the Midlands, from Bath to Liverpool, equipped with maps, notebooks, and knapsacks.

Early in 1883 W. Satchell and Co. published a small, handwritten book by Saml. Cliall White called *Forgotten Ballads,* or *Bedlam Ballads and Straitwaistcoat Stories, Part I.* Saml. Cliall White is an anagram of William Satchell, who was the real author. The contents are a prose tale called "The Carbuncle: A Spanish Legend," and two fantastic ballads called "The Phantom Ship: A Legend of the Something-or-Other Main," and "Some Account of the Battle between Henry Fitzleopold Cheveril Toots and De Liegh de Clarence Brown." These juvenilia are of interest now chiefly to show Satchell's youthful gift for burlesque writing.

His real debut came with his second book, *Will o' The Wisp,* published in hard covers on October 10, 1883, without any author's name on the title page. It was dedicated to Allan Fea and is a substantial volume of ballads and prose tales. Satchell shows himself here to be strongly under the sway of German romanticism, and parts of this collection may well have been written while he was at Heidelberg. Although Fea saw in the book the influence of Thomas Hood and Edgar Allan Poe, the prose tales, concerned wtih supernatural events and set mainly in old English castles and manors, owe much as well to Hoffmann and Hawthorne.

Despite the competent nature of the writing within the romantic-gothic genre which Satchell had chosen, the book fell victim to what can only be called the aversion to Poe's work which existed in England and Europe among some critics. So the reviewer of *Will o' The Wisp* in the *Academy* said of its anonymous author: "We should not be sorry to see him again in verse, but we trust never more to have to read a collection of prose tales such as those he has given us."

It is difficult to understand now this condemnation of Satchell's tales, which are at least the equal of his early poetry. But one effect was to make him give up writing fiction for the next ten years. He continued to write poetry and poetic drama, without success, until at last the great decision was made in the Satchell home—William must emigrate.

Satchell's mood at this critical time is revealed in letters to Allan Fea. On August 8, 1883, he writes:

I think I was born to be a torture to myself and others. At present there is a cloud before me so thick, that of the future I can form no conjecture whatever. Everything appears to be drifting slowly away and leaving me—only the cloud thickens and blots out the last vestige of hope and faith. I believe in *nothing*—neither Man nor God, nor Devil. . . . My stories are all the thought of an instant, and the fevered work of a few hours. While I am engaged upon them, I think of nothing else, and for many hours before and after they are written, they are to me true—truer than anything on earth. I think then it will not be possible to live on the work of my brain, because in the first place I could not produce enough to keep me from starving;

and in the second I see no chance of a beginning—although I do distinctly see a chance of an ending.[1]

He was not in fact able to make that desired beginning until ten years later, in Auckland, New Zealand. His later view of life is foreshadowed in the following sentences from another letter to Fea.

My highest ambition is not to become famous or to write books, but to dream—surely little enough. I am debarred from even this. "Charge !" cries a voice of Progress and they who would stand still, and look back with beating hearts and tearful eyes upon the past, fall and are trodden to the dust. Still it is well, for the hearts of men are the rungs of the ladder of God. Sometimes we would wish that the ascending foot were less heavy.

Again he writes:

Well, you know me, I am conceited, crotchety, sometimes (perhaps always) idiotic in my letters, stiff as a weathercock, and as high as the clouds, but I think I have often descended as deep in self-contempt as I have risen in self-glory.

On November 5, 1884, when his father removed him from the publishing firm, he wrote to Fea:

I observe I am to be superseded altogether. Do you know anyone who requires a clerk in a rag and bone house, if so I rely on your good word. There is nothing much brighter for one. O for a thousand pounds and a hovel in the heart of a forest that I might fly away and be at rest.

He took action to achieve his latest ambition by sailing for New Zealand and setting up his tent in a block of four hundred acres of puriri forest situated in a remote, mountainous gorge of the Waima valley. It was about as far from London and the Voice of Progress as a man could get in those days.

His rejection of modern, Western civilization was an expression of the deepest trend in his nature. He came to identify himself in his fiction largely with the New Zealand past, with the wilderness and with the Maori point of view. It was an inclination shared by his brother Tom, who went to live in Japan and married a Japanese girl.

Satchell's preparations for the life of a pioneer settler were meagre. After a period of illness, he spoke in March, 1886 of spending a fortnight in a Hampshire farmhouse, to pick up a few hints on farming practice, or else of going to Brockenhurst in the New Forest, to "see something of the timber felling." At any rate he left London on the S.S. *Arawa* on May 21, 1886, aged twenty-six, with his partner Elmer J. Brown, who was selected by placing an advertisement in the London *Daily News*. His cousin Frank Tomlinson and his brother Tom followed later.

A few days before the *Arawa* sailed, there appeared in London bookshops Thomas Hardy's novel, *The Mayor of Casterbridge*. Satchell probably took a copy with him. The example of Hardy, especially in *The Woodlanders*, helped him to formulate his own early novels, though the two men's vision of life and artistic aims were different.

What was Satchell like at this time? Physically he was of small build, about five feet six inches tall, slim, with thick brown wavy hair, high forehead, wide-set blue eyes, large nose and jaw with a drooping moustache. He wore a velvet jacket and a cravat instead of a tie. His health was not good. Emotionally, his failure as an author in London had disturbed him. Intellectually, since he had been born into an age of skepticism, he found it hard to believe in anything in spite of a strong desire to believe. At Heidelberg he was bound to have read Goethe and Schiller with deep respect, and he probably became acquainted there with nineteenth century German philosophy.

Now what were the reasons for his failure in London? The period after his return from Germany—that is, from 1879 to 1886—was one of widespread economic depression, when England was ablaze with new thought, and society was being shaken by the socialist uprising. Why was he not actively involved in this ferment of activity? Furthermore, a dozen talented novelists were writing in England, yet he had moved timorously on the fringes of London's literary life. Obviously he needed the stimulus of a fresh environment before he could develop.

One reason for his revulsion and flight from the London of his birth may have been the notorious decadence at that time of English upperclass life. For instance, as he left Hampstead, a series of sexual scandals had already begun to rock London society. The Sir Charles Dilke-Mrs. Crawford case was soon followed by that of Parnell and Kitty O'Shea, and also by the sensational Lady Colin Campbell divorce. Nevertheless, in leaving Europe he was giving up, in the year 1886, a very great deal that was valuable and stimulating in art and literature.

George Eliot had recently died, but Thomas Hardy, George Meredith, Robert Louis Stevenson, George Gissing, and Bernard Shaw (as a young novelist) were all writing. Shaw was also deeply involved in the socialist revival as a pamphleteer and street orator. Robert Browning was writing his last poems in London, where the Americans Henry James and Bret Harte were being lionised. Henry Irving and Ellen Terry dominated the theatrical world. Millais and Burne-Jones, Whistler and Sargent, were supreme in art. In Paris, although Turgenev and Flaubert were dead, Zola, Maupassant, Daudet, the Goncourt brothers, Bourget, Loti and Coppée were at work. Ibsen's plays were being translated into German, and two years earlier in America Mark Twain had published *The Adventures of Huckleberry Finn.*

Satchell says nothing in his letters of this artistic activity, nor of the socialist upheaval that was going on in England. Was he present at the Piccadilly Riots of February, 1886? He must have known of the appalling living conditions of London's poor people. Yet judging by his letters written from Hampstead, the mob violence in London's streets, the meetings of the Democratic Federation, the Socialist League, the Fabian Society—the writings of Marx and Engels, of Shaw and Sidney Webb—even the meetings of the English Positivist Society—apparently meant nothing to him.

He does, however, appear to have taken more interest in current scientific and philosophical ideas; it is possible that his father was an agnostic, like the agnostic father-figures in his novels, Major Milward and Purcell. He probably took with him to New Zealand Darwin's *The Origin of Species,* as well as the more conventional volumes of Shakespeare and Wordsworth. His novels reveal that he must have read John Stuart Mill's *Three Essays on Religion,* and Spencer's *First Principles,* which was published in 1893. In 1894 Annie Besant toured New Zealand and lectured in Auckland, and he was presumably acquainted with her attacks on the accepted role of women in Victorian society. He had surely read Olive Schreiner, whose articles were

appearing in the *New Zealand Graphic* at the same time that
he was writing for that weekly magazine himself.

Clearly his very strong ideals about the betterment of society, instead of being channelled into the current socialist thinking, were converted to a belief in the growth of democratic
egalitarianism, which he soon observed in the pioneering community of Hokianga County. He was a disciple of Bentham,
Mill, and Owen rather than of Marx and Engels. He described
himself as "a democrat of democrats" and his novels reveal a
frontier spirit in nineteenth century New Zealand society very
similar to that in the United States at that time.

His criticisms of New Zealand society were not based on "class
war" doctrines, but were an attack on "cash-book morality," inhumanity in church and government, hypocrisy, poverty, and
racial prejudice. His fictional heroes are handsome, stalwart
young creatures, men of good education who have stepped outside society for one reason or another, but who end up by marrying back into established society, or who continue to challenge it until it destroys them.

His restless, probing intellectualism focussed on the crumbling
of religious belief which was a common subject in Victorian
literature. This is reflected in *The Toll of the Bush* and to a
lesser extent in *The Greenstone Door*. Into another novel, *The
Elixir of Life*, he projected current ideas for the betterment
of society through science and medicine.

He approved the agnosticism brought forward by men like
T. H. Huxley, Mill, and Spencer, especially where they attacked
the doctrines of the existence of God and the literal accuracy of
the Bible and the soul's immortality. Thus he asks: "If all that
tremendous tomorrow be for us a silence, even as the tremendous yesterday is a silence, where then shall be the recompense
for what life denies us? Hope, faith—what are they but shadows
compared with the substance we shall have missed?" This was
his agonized question in *The Toll of the Bush*, which shows how
close his thought comes at times to Positivism. Yet he believed
it was wrong to follow the Comtist idea that science can elim-
inate the metaphysical instinct.

He imagined that when science had gone as far as possible
in revealing the nature of the universe it would ultimately be

faced with the unknowable, so that the sense of wonder must
still exist.

Science recognizes that at some remote date she may reach a point
where her tests will no longer meet with response, where the abyss
will not yield to the plummet, and all the accumulated knowledge of
the ages cannot carry her forward one single step.

So despite the toughness of his agnosticism, the main current
of his novels is more of a Platonic idealism, leading to a pan-
theistic nature-worship.

He says much about cosmic questions in his novels, and he
saw in his virgin New Zealand bush country a manifestation of
the absolute. He saw in the bush unexplained and unexplored
depths of power and mystery, so that like some divine force
it took its toll of those who destroyed it. His life in the bush
also inspired him with a deep fatalism. He saw evil not only as
a result of social maladjustment, but as the product of cosmic
necessity too powerful for human society to resist. For him the
pitiless fates which had dominated the world of Homer and
Aeschylus also operated in the pioneer settlements on the
Hokianga.

2 *Hokianga Years*

When Satchell emigrated, New Zealand life had hardly begun.
It was less than fifty years old by the accepted dating from the
Treaty of Waitangi of 1840. His long voyage on the *Arawa* inspired him with new courage and hope, and restored his health.
He wrote to Allan Fea: "there is the new land with its promise
to rouse one ... I thought of all this as I crossed the equator
and went down the world into the southern hemisphere, and
sailed under new stars." He fell in love with New Zealand immediately and his enthusiastic letter to Fea included the phrase,
"a beautiful land it is."

After taking lodgings at Arawa Cottage in Spring Street, Free-
man's Bay, Auckland, he and Brown, equipped with survey maps,
went to inspect land available for settlement near Whangarei.
Here he made his first acquaintance with the bush:

Masses of trees covered with parasites, with ferns of the most beautiful description running up the trunks, and supplejacks binding them round with ropes of iron. Down in the dim gullies, where a narrow stream half choked by vegetation can be heard tinkling over the stones, the air is humid and warm as that of a hot house. . . . For the main part saving now and again the snapping of a branch there is dead silence, a sort of black quiet. . . .

His novelist's eye was already noting and recording details, for he found the people of the new land as fascinating as its natural wonders.

You would be amused at the way people ride here. It is no unusual sight to see a little girl galloping a big horse with sixteen pounds of meat on the pommel of her saddle and a bag of potatoes under one arm. . . . All the girls I must tell you are pretty, some, especially the children, beautiful. Walking this evening (Saturday) down Queen Street . . . I was astonished at the incessant stream of pretty girls: blooming young creatures, well made and walking gracefully.

His interest in New Zealand's Maori inhabitants also provoked sharp observations.

They are a fine, intelligent race, and can beat the white man sometimes in a bargain. . . . I have seen them standing in small knots peeping into Auckland shops, and commenting softly to one another in their flowing tongue on the wonders that met their gaze. Their fate is a hard one—they are too slow for the white man, can neither stand against him, nor walk with him.

Although his views on the Maoris changed, his sympathy for them always remained, and these vivid early impressions formed the basis of his treatment of them in his novels and stories.

The Whangarei land did not suit Satchell and Brown, but they met there John Lundon, who owned a store and hotel at Rawene in Hokianga County and had at this time just started his land settlement scheme in Hokianga. Their meeting was a turning point in Satchell's life, for Lundon was a brilliant man with a remarkable past, one of the early pioneers whom Satchell later idealized in his novels. He persuaded Satchell to follow him north to Rawene.

The Hokianga River drains a sub-tropical region whose great

historical and literary interest must have attracted Satchell strongly. The river is a blue, mile-wide estuary indenting the North Auckland peninsula across from the Bay of Islands, where American whaling ships had refitted long before British rule was established. Following Kupe's discovery of New Zealand at Hokianga in 1050, the main parties of Maori colonists arrived from Tahiti and Rarotonga in 1350 or thereabouts, and their descendants at Hokianga, a mixture of the Ngapuhi and Rarawa tribes, were a docile, friendly people.

The first white man in Hokianga was probably Jackie Marmon, an escaped convict from Australia who was called Cannibal Jack, because he allegedly took part in the feast on his dead companions' bodies after they had been captured by the Maoris. But all other white arrivals lived there in peace. Following the missionaries Kendall and King, Marsden and Pompallier, came authors and artists such as Augustus Earle and Edward Markham, the eccentric Charles de Thierry, self-styled king of New Zealand, with his retinue, and the Maori scholar, John White.

The most celebrated early Hokianga author was a mysterious Irishman, F. E. Maning, who married the sister of a chief called Hauraki, and wrote his account of life on the river in the classic, *Old New Zealand* (1863). Many other strange men lived on the river in the old days—idealists and visionaries, artists and poets, runaway seamen, escaped convicts, old soldiers, adventurers, traders, scholars, builders, and remittance men. Although the 1886 census revealed a total population of 578,482 whites and 41,961 Maoris in New Zealand, the Hokianga proportions were 2,364 Maoris and only 572 whites, of whom 201 had Maori wives. At the large Maori settlement in the Waima Valley where Satchell and Brown settled, the only other whites were the local schoolteacher and his wife, Mr. and Mrs. Hill. Satchell wrote to Fea:

I am now living in a tent shaded with palm leaves, pitched in a small glade in the midst of virgin forest . . . we are clearing a few acres for orange trees, our intention being to plant in glades of several acres in extent, and not, as is too generally the case here, to remove the whole forest with fire.

Next to the Hills, Satchell's closest friend in the district was

John Webster, who served as a model for his character Major Milward in *The Toll of the Bush*. Webster was born in 1818 at Montrose, Scotland, went to Australia where he took part in overland cattle drives, and came to Hokianga in 1841. He fought with Maning, Marmon, and others in Heke's War of 1844-45, when Hone Heke cut down the British flag at the Bay of Islands, partly, so it is said, at the instigation of Yankee whalers. After this, Webster and John Logan Campbell (whose *Poenamo* is another classic tale of the old days) went to the California diggings during the gold rush of 1849. Finally Webster settled at Opononi on a 700-acre sheep and cattle station which appears in *The Toll of the Bush* as "Wairangi." He wrote two books himself, *The Last Cruise of the "Wanderer"* and *Reminiscences of an Old Settler,* and his friendship meant a great deal to Satchell in the years of struggle ahead.

Satchell has said little about his marriage to Susan Bryers in 1889. But Susan was the granddaughter of another famous old Hokianga settler, Joseph Bryers. Born in Liverpool about 1816, Bryers came to the Bay of Islands around 1835 and married Kohu, daughter of the chief Whareumu, who was known to the missionaries as "King George." Whareumu's wife (Kohu's mother) was the daughter of Kawiti, whose name stands at the head of all those chiefs who signed the Treaty of Waitangi. Kohu was famous for having brought Kawiti into the Flagstaff War or Hone Heke's War on Heke's side in an incident described as "The Rising of Kawiti" in *The Life of Henry Williams.*

A further account of the family into which Satchell married is given by James Grey, who describes his arrival at Bryers' Hotel in Rawene and a meeting with old Mr. Bryers and Susan's uncle, who

. . . speaks both Maori and English fluently, and from his mother inherits considerable rank amongst the hapu to which he belongs. It was this same Mr. Bryers who at the late assemblage at Kopua, as one of the representatives of the Ngapuhi nation, made such a forcible speech on the side of the Government.[2]

This was John, brother of Susan's father George.

Susan was seventeen when Satchell married her. She had two sisters, Catherine and Margaret, born at Herd's Point (Rawene)

in 1866 and 1867. Susan, however, was born at Thames in 1872, toward the end of the first gold rush. Satchell wrote two stories about the goldfields—one concerning a lost reef at Thames called "The Yellow Dwarf," and another about an abandoned mine in "Wilkes' Sanatorium."

Today Hokianga is a pastoral county, but the earliest white settlers sold kauri spars for sailing ships, milled timber, and dug for kauri gum. The gumfields form the setting of Satchell's novel *The Land of the Lost* and his short story, "From a Northern Gumfield." Both reveal practical knowledge of life on the Taheke and Kawerua fields, and suggest that he worked on the gumfields himself in the intervals of felling the bush on his Waima tract of land. James Clendon of Hokianga, New Zealand's first American Counsul, was the man who collected and sent the first kauri gum to England where it came to be sold for use in varnish-making. A gumdigger's life was precarious, but it attracted many unemployed workers in the depression of the 1880s.

Satchell's orange-growing venture was based on the advice of an Italian named Federli, who lectured and wrote to show how subtropical fruits could be grown in Hokianga. In 1886 several "village settlements" were formed in the district and thousands of apple trees were distributed by the Agriculture Department. Wild cattle which roamed the bush destroyed the seedlings, and most of these settlements failed. Many smallholders abandoned their land and worked as bush-fallers or on the gumfields. Satchell used their experiences in *The Toll of the Bush* and in his story "The Great Unemployed Scheme."

Although economic conditions in New Zealand were so bad in the 80s that the outflow of settlers to Australia exceeded the inflow from Britain, and many large farmers and businessmen went bankrupt, Satchell's venture as a pioneer failed for the additional reason that he could not get a freehold title to his land. He had moved in without waiting to learn if the Maori who "sold" him the land was its legal owner. Yet the outdoor life suited him. In 1890 their first child, Edith, was born in the house he built at Waima. He also built a settlers' hall in the valley and founded a cricket club at Rawene called the Wanderers.

After his father's death in 1887 his brother Tom and cousin Frank Tomlinson had come out to work with him, but by 1891 the whole enterprise had collapsed, and the partners broke up. Brown went to Australia and Tom returned to England from where he later emigrated to Japan. Frank vanished from sight to reappear in Satchell's life in Auckland in 1911.

For a while Satchell worked as a storekeeper at one of the nearby settlements—Taheke, Rawene, or Opononi. The life of a storekeeper is featured in both his Hokianga novels and in several short stories, so apparently this obscure part of his experience made a strong impression on him. But it was no solution to his financial problems. By this time he had decided to resume his life as a writer. In 1892 he moved to Auckland, where his son Tom was born in the suburb of Parnell. It was hard to find work, and when his money ran out he sent Susan and the babies back to live with her aunt in Hokianga, in April, 1893.

He went to stay with J. C. Webster at Cheltenham Beach, North Shore, from where he wrote a desperate appeal to Sir George Grey, who had been long since removed from his governorship of New Zealand by the British and was now the leader of the Liberal Party, though he ceased to appear in Parliament after the 1892 session. The appeal was probably suggested by John Webster, who had known Grey during Heke's War and had also met him in London. The letter sets out Satchell's grievance over the loss of his land title, for which he blamed the government, and states that although he had brought New Zealand the benefits of his own ability as a "small capitalist" and an "industrious man," he had received in exchange nothing but starvation. He included samples of his latest writings, the poem "Hinemoa" (based on the tale in Grey's book of Maori legends) and a verse drama called *Hemeroma,* which (although it was never published) handled in verse form the same theme which became the basis of his novel *The Greenstone Door:* the clash between white man and Maori.

On May 19, 1893, he wrote to Allan Fea giving details of his recent work, notably a short novel set in New Zealand and titled *The Cadet,* and a four-act tragedy, *The Nihilist,* neither of which was published. As he said to Fea:

The stories I have sent home to my brother do not go off. Nobody will take up the poems. I am head over ears in debt and there is no employment of a permanent nature to be had. I have lately been

employed on a novel, but I have now so little confidence in myself
as a writer that the offer of work of almost any character, and at any
rate of remuneration, would be sufficient to lure me from literature
forever.

But at least he had made that beginning which ten years before
he had despaired of ever seeing. It was no longer important to
him that his appeal to Grey brought no reply, because a flood
of poetry, prose, and drama was now pouring from his pen.

3 Short Story Writer

The reasons for Satchell's great upsurge of creative energy
in the early 90s were partly a feeling of desperation, partly a
lack of any other employment, but also a sense of personal freedom which lifted him out of the bitterness of his failure in
Hokianga. He was happily married. The new land suited his
temperament; there was no question of returning to England.
His debts and his poverty acted as a spur. He was completely
on his own. He had no regular address at this period and his
letters were written from the C.P.O., Auckland. He may even
have been sleeping in the parks along with Auckland's hundreds
of other unemployed that summer, 1893. He wrote to Fea, on
December 1st, and said he had christened his third child, whom
he had not yet seen, Allan in his honor.

He was encouraged to write for the *Graphic*, a weekly subsidiary of the *Auckland Star*, by its editor Wilfred Rathbone.
The *Graphic*, founded in 1890 by Henry Brett as the *New Zealand Graphic, Ladies' Journal and Youth Companion*, made a
feature of fiction and poetry in its pages, and between January
and September 1894 ten poems by "W.S." appeared. In November the long poem "In Memoriam" by Samuel Cliall White com-
memorated the wreck of the *Wairarapa* on Great Barrier Island
three weeks earlier, and there were ten stories by Samuel Cliall
White in the *Graphic* between June 1894 and January 1896. Further material under other nom-de-plumes may also have been
written by Satchell.

The first of the stories, "The Great Unemployed Scheme," is
a satire, a little after the manner of Mark Twain, on the harsh
living conditions of New Zealand's bush settlers. The savagery
of this story, though partly concealed from its newspaper read-

ers by the lightly humorous tone, reveals the slow, subtle changes which had been made in Satchell's personality by his transfer from a sheltered London life to the primitive New Zealand backblocks. His removal from a dilettante English milieu to an outdoor, pioneer existence had hardened him and toughened his attitude to life. Exile and poverty had done their work, but there is little self-pity or resentment in the story. As always he is urbane. Yet it is clear that from being a foppish aesthete he had become a writer of purpose.

It is interesting that even his handwriting had changed since he came to New Zealand, becoming smaller, neater, firmer, and showing greater determination and force. What experiences he had endured to be able to hammer out the basic truths of human society in his fiction from now on can only be inferred. But the quality of his writing continued to improve after "The Great Unemployed Scheme," which marks the turning point in his career as a writer. Social criticism was to prove his real vocation. Although in his novels he made a pretense of writing pleasant romances, he repudiated or challenged conventional behavior and the socially-accepted view of things in practically every word he wrote.

The sale of his stories and poems to the *Graphic* could not have provided him with enough to live on, but it did restore his confidence in his ability. Most of his *Graphic* stories were illustrated by C. Stickley, whose drawings for "From A Northern Gumfield" showing the two gumfield mates in wide-brimmed hats beside their horses, with a crude hut and a group of watching Maoris in the background, express the atmosphere of the period. Line and half-tone illustrations of stories and poems were very common in antipodean magazines at that time, and were most lavish in the Sydney *Bulletin,* which employed several very capable artists.

In 1895 he continued to sell stories and poems to the *Graphic.* Although he had now abandoned *The Cadet,* he may have begun work on *The Land of the Lost.* Two other events of major importance occurred that year. First, the family were reunited: Susan and the three young children left her aunt's place in Rawene and came down to Auckland, where they all moved into a rented cottage at Ponsonby. In addition, the second Thames gold rush, which began in January, enabled Satchell to make his first real money as an Auckland sharebroker.

The story of the Thames goldfields goes back to 1852, when a wandering digger named Charles Ring prospected the whole of the Coromandel Range from Cape Colville south to Mount Te Aroha, finding gold all the way. The first Thames rush started in 1867 with the famous Shotover Mine in Kuranui Creek. As news of the bonanza spread, diggers poured in from Otago, the West Coast, Australia, and California. Next year was the peak period with 18,000 on the diggings, but the boom gradually collapsed during the world-wide depression of 1873-93. The second Thames rush started in January 1895 with the discovery of the Hauraki bonanza at Coromandel, and lasted till 1899. There was a third rush when the Waiotahi bonanza was brought in during 1905-07.

Susan had been born on the diggings in the first rush, and Satchell saw the new boom as his chance. He became a sharebroker in Auckland, where most of the shareholders in the Thames mines lived. The importation of large crushing plants to Thames and the introduction of the cyanide process, with the backing of English financiers, created a feeling of confidence. In October, 1895, when 164 mining companies had been registered on the Thames field, Albert Cuff wrote in the *Graphic:*

In Auckland the activity on the Stock Exchange is great and the amount of money changing hands every hour very large indeed. The brokers are making large sums daily. . . . The tradespeople in Auckland, I may say, are beginning to complain that the whole of the money of the people is being spent in shares.

Because seats on the Stock Exchange were limited, outside brokers including Satchell formed their own association called the Free Exchange. Daily auctions of mining scrip were held, and the rival exchanges each had three calls daily. A reporter noted that "the values of shares advance and recede in a manner most embarrassing for the average speculator, and most enriching for the brokers." [3]

By 1900, after the boom ended, Satchell had enough money to move to a big, luxuriously furnished house in Grange Road,

Mount Roskill, where he worked hard at *The Land of the Lost.*
In 1897 their fifth child, named Alice, had been born in Ponsonby. In the same year he received £300 from his father's estate. Everything was now in his favor.

Given such prospects, he decided to publish his better poems
from the *Graphic* and other newspapers in a book called *Patriotic
and Other Poems.* It was issued in 1900 by the Brett Printing
and Publishing Co. a slim book with a yellow cardboard cover
carrying a black and red drawing of the Union Jack. Each copy
was numbered and signed by the author and it sold at two
shillings. The first seven poems are "patriotically" about the
Boer War, in which New Zealand's Rough Riders were already
fighting alongside British and Canadian troops. They are jour-
neyman verses—vigorous, undistinguished, jingoistic, tub-thump-
ing, often crude, and showing a strong influence of Rudyard
Kipling. The best poems in the book are the short lyrics, odes,
and bush ballads on New Zealand themes, and several satirical
poems attacking the mechanistic-scientific view of the universe.

The book was well received. The Wellington *Evening Post*
said that Satchell was "entitled to a high place among Australian poets." The *Graphic* review drew attention to "The Ballad of Stuttering Jim," which was "as powerful and dramatic
a story in verse as we have read." A more adverse comment came
two years later from brother Tom, who was now editor of the
Japan Herald: "I did not like the war ballads, the fact being
that I detest Kipling . . . as much as I abhor Imperialism." By
that time, however, Satchell had practically given up writing
poetry and had published his first novel. But the poems are still
living proof of that conjunction of imperialism and romanticism
which T. S. Eliot writes about in *The Sacred Wood.*

4   *Links with Australia*

One of the best poems in the *Patriotic* collection was "The
Ballad of Stuttering Jim." It had been first published in Australia
in the Sydney *Bulletin,* and it so impressed the *Bulletin's* celebrated editor, A. G. Stephens, that he included it in his anthol-
ogy *The Bulletin Reciter.* Satchell was the only New Zealander
besides Arthur H. Adams to be represented. He thus takes his

place alongside Henry Lawson, Banjo Paterson and others of the Australian "bush" school of writers in the *Bulletin,* who expressed the first feelings of nationalism and the desire of the two colonies to break free from Britain.

Bulletin prose sketches and ballads were mainly about the digger, the bushman, the shearer, the bullocky, and the swagger who were the archetypes of the egalitarian society which had grown out of pioneer conditions and the gold rushes of the Sixties. It was probably through studying the methods and themes of the *Bulletin* writers that Satchell found his best approach to New Zealand material. The ideal of "mateship" expounded so frequently in Henry Lawson's stories, which was a genuine factor of colonial life where the inhospitable environment forced collective action on the pioneers, finds persistent expression in Satchell's work.

In a letter to the *Bulletin* Satchell praised New Zealand hospitality and contrasted it with conditions in England. "The Englishman of today lives on the credit accumulated by his ancestors: he is swollen by conceit beyond all tolerance. Somebody will stick a bayonet in him one of these days, and the gas will escape in a hurry." [4] But the aggressive independence of this letter does not appear to the same extent in his novels; by contrast with the larrikinism of Joe Wilson and his mates in Lawson's stories, Satchell's heroes are often chivalrous, well-spoken, and virtuous gentlemen. He is thus less like the native-born Lawson than those English exiles in Australia—such as Marcus Clarke or Adam Lindsay Gordon—who wrote some of the best early Australian novels and poems yet were essentially observers from outside with a strong English element in their work.

Much of his new feeling that he was now a New Zealander instead of an Englishman was expressed in the pages of the weekly literary paper which he edited, published, and largely wrote himself in 1901. He called it *The Maorilander,* thus borrowing the current *Bulletin* term for a New Zealander. Its first issue came out on February 8th, a few days after the birth of his sixth child, a daughter named Mary. In it he stated editorially: "We believe there is need in New Zealand for a paper which, while not being a repository of news, yet in the main concerns itself with matters of colonial interest." He wanted to encourage new writers "of a literature striving to assert itself in a new land," and offered prizes to contributors.

The editor in fact was the chief contributor. "The Stone Stable Mystery" was a seven-part serial from his pen, not completed because *The Maorilander* ceased publication after its seventh issue on March 29th. Other sketches and stories by Satchell include extracts from his novel *The Toll of the Bush,* which he was writing at the same time. He also contributed poems.

Despite such a gesture towards literary independence, however, he still needed the English market, and English publishers, in order to get his novels into print. All four of them, beginning with *The Land of the Lost* next year, were published in London first of all. He also placed stories and articles in London magazines such as *National Review* and *Grand Magazine* through his literary agent, J. B. Pinker.

His Australian links included dramatic work. In April 1908, J. C. Williamson's of Sydney acknowledged receipt of his manuscript play *The Divided Note,* but it was never produced on the stage, either in Australia or New Zealand. Other attempts at playwriting about this time were equally unsuccessful, though there was later on talk of making a film out of his *Bulletin* poem, "The Ballad of Stuttering Jim." None of his short stories was reprinted in book form, and the first of his prose works to appear in hard covers since the English tales in *Will o' the Wisp* was the novel on which he had worked for so long.

Nevertheless, his connection with Australian writers through the pages of the *Bulletin* was of very real importance to his work. In particular he drew much inspiration from the example of Henry Lawson's stories, and at one time was actually in position to have met Lawson: the early summer of 1893, when he had no fixed address and was writing to Allan Fea from c/o C.P.O.—when he was one of Auckland's unemployed, many of whom were sleeping in the parks. At this time Henry Lawson, aged twenty-six—seven years younger than Satchell—arrived in Auckland, practically unknown yet as a writer. Himself out of work, he had been driven from Australia with others by the 1893 depression, which was the climax of a series of bad seasons. He wrote the story "Coming Across" about his voyage from Sydney among English immigrants or new chums; and

Australians seeking work in "Maoriland," as he called it—chiefly tradesmen, laborers, clerks, and bagmen. They too had been driven from Australia by the hard times there, and were glad, no doubt, to get away. They saw New Zealand as a Promised Land, but as the final sentence of "Coming Across" has it: "Pity we couldn't go to sea and sail away for ever, and never see land any more—or, at least, not till better and brighter days— if they ever come."

There is no record, however, that there was any meeting between these two men, whose future careers were to be so fruitful for Australian and New Zealand literature. How revealing it might have been if such a meeting had taken place, and one of the men had kept notes of what they said to each other, as W. B. Yeats so humbly and shrewdly did of his meeting with the young James Joyce. But of course neither knew what the other was likely to become. It was a time of chaos, almost universal poverty, confused living, and little hope for the future. Yet it was also the time when the first faint stirrings of independence grew in the Australian and New Zealand consciousness, and a sense of national identity was being hammered out hot from the fires of bitterness and failure.

After three months with the New Zealand unemployed, Lawson found a job at a sawmill in the Hutt Valley, where he stayed briefly, and later as a telegraph linesman in Nelson and Palmerston North. In June 1894, when Lawson returned to Australia, Satchell's first New Zealand story appeared—"The Great Unemployed Scheme." During Lawson's second New Zealand visit of 1807-08, Satchell was writing steadily, and he read Lawson's stories. Though he does not accept all the dark Lawson despondency, he does evoke in his Hokianga novels and stories a kindred mood of the desperate nature of everyday life among ordinary people in those bleak days.

The slump marked Satchell's outlook on life as permanently as Lawson's even harsher experiences did. Thus it is not surprising that the lonely gumfields characters of *The Land of the Lost* resemble Mitchell, Joe Wilson, Dave Regan, and the rest of Lawson's people—the professional wanderers of his great fictional world. Bogg of Gebung, Lawson's derelict remittance man, could have been the inspiration for Bart in *The Land of the Lost*, while Doc Wilde, the Yankee alcoholic, anticipates Sven

Anderson in *The Toll of the Bush*. Yet Satchell was working from independent experiences.

Satchell and Lawson both write of the bitterness of exile, of the loneliness of the human condition in the colonial world of the 1890s; both make use of the theme of two men bearing the burden of a painful or guilty past. Lawson's handling of vernacular in a collection like *Joe Wilson's Mates* appears to lead directly to much that is so impressively colloquial and familiar in *The Land of the Lost* and the rest of Satchell's fiction. But the differences between the two men's methods are greater than the similarities.

5   *The Land of the Lost*

When *The Land of the Lost* was published in England in March, 1902, Satchell was forty-two. He had worked hard for many years to produce his novel and it was well received in London. The *Athenaeum* said on March 22nd that it

. . . lacks the dash and cleverness of the best American fiction yet has more "nature sense"; more primitive depth and breadth, more of the quality which goes to make the work of Mr. Thomas Hardy great . . . the author is imbued with a strong appreciative sense of the bigness and beauty and mystery of nature.

This was good, but by contrast the New Zealand reception was disappointing. A brief notice in the *Auckland Star* of July 21st was not unfavorable, but it said very little more than that "Mr. Satchell's descriptions are vivid and picturesque, and he is gifted with the art of telling a story well," and that the novel "depicted a phase of life as singular in its marked characteristics as those digger scenes in California which Bret Harte made familiar to the outside world." Satchell had never met Bret Harte, who had died a few weeks earlier, and despite similarities in themes there is little internal evidence to show that he was influenced much if at all by Harte's work.

But why was the value of his novel as a contribution to New Zealand literature so little appreciated at the time? Alan Mulgan, a poet and novelist, commented on this many years later.

To Auckland people the gumfields were something at their doors.

Literally at their doors, for there was a notorious gumdiggers' camp at Henderson, a few miles out of the city. . . . But they were not interested; it was too near home. Romance was something that came from the African spaces or the Hudson Bay Territory, not from the other side of one's own hills.[5]

Be that as it may, it is a fact that the novel had few readers in New Zealand until it was reprinted in 1938.

If *The Land of the Lost* is the smoothest and lightest of Satchell's books, it has all the freshness of a first novel. It contrasts society at Rawene (called Parawai in the book), the Hokianga township of 1890 presented in all its thinness and conventionality, with the primitive life of the gumfield and the bush. It includes three idealized portraits of young New Zealanders in Hugh Clifford, a rugged sheepfarmer and an outdoors type; Wilfred Hamilton, a doctor who has just taken his medical degree in England and is clever, poised, and wholly admirable; and Esther Hamilton, his beautiful, auburn-haired cousin. There is much witty talk in the manner of Henry James, much dark brooding in the gumfield sections, much affection in the picture of Maori life and in descriptions of bush country.

What is least credible is the coincidence that Upmore, the sinister proprietor of the Scarlet Man bush pub, should be the half-brother (having changed his name and secretly emigrated to New Zealand) of young Clifford, the heir who has come to the gumfield to get away from the importunities of his mother, who wants him to share the inheritance with another, younger, brother. It is only by ignoring this coincidence and concentrating on the minor characters and incidents that one sees the book's artistry.

During the three years after *The Land of the Lost*, Satchell worked solely on his second novel. However, in 1904 he sent two stories to the *Graphic*. One was the old story, "The Stone Stable Mystery"; the other, "The Divided Note," was also apparently old work. The hero of both stories is a character called Hazlett or Haslett; in the first he is a police detective and in the second a scientist.

Both were published anonymously—an indication that he did not think highly of them and used them only to get money to help feed his family. "The Divided Note," which came out on

January 2, 1904, is a narrative version of the play he later sent to J. C. Williamson's in Sydney. It has a North Auckland setting, several gumdigger characters, and contains a reference to a Hokianga digger mentioned in *The Land of the Lost,* Sandy George. The general style suggests that it was originally cast in dramatic form, as does the fact that it is printed in four titled parts—"The Dead Man on the Sands," "The Girl of the Cliffs," "The House on the Headland," and "The Migration of the Godwits." On April 23rd, April 30th, May 7th, and May 14th, the *Graphic* printed "The Stone Stable Mystery" in four parts, complete for the first time. "The Divided Note" was later retitled "The House on the Headland" and sent without success to J. B. Pinker in London.

6   *The Toll of the Bush*

Satchell continued living at Mount Roskill, where his seventh child, a son named Hugh, was born in 1903, and his eighth, a son named George, in 1905. His new novel, *The Toll of the Bush,* came out in October of that year as No. 500 in Macmillan's Colonial Library. It was issued in paper covers as well as in boards, and went into a second impression. The tone of the book is more somber than in *The Land of the Lost,* with a deeper sense of doubt in its portrayal of pioneer life on the Hokianga. The new contrast is between the bush settlement where the brothers Geoffrey and Robert Hernshaw are hacking their farm out of the wilderness, and the big sheep and cattle station of "Wairangi" at Opononi (called Rivermouth in the book), and an unnamed township which is again Rawene. The events are dated about 1900 but the situation at Hokianga is actually that of about 1890.

Again Satchell's work was better received abroad than at home. The London *Athenaeum* of October 28th said: "This is a colonial novel of remarkable merit and distinction. It has a rounded completeness, a full and broad humanity, which are by no means characteristic of contemporary fiction." It was "a story full of real characterization" in which the New Zealand "atmosphere and background are sketched in masterly style." This reviewer added that contemporary fiction "dealing with Australasia consists too often of intensely pessimistic sincerity or amiable, optimistic twaddle. Here, however, is a story of the golden middle path."

By contrast the *Auckland Star* of December 2nd damned it with faint praise: "The simple life of the North Auckland settler with its deadly round of commonplace duties, may appear an unlikely sphere wherein to look for soul-stirring romance." The reviewer showed only a limited understanding of the book, though he conceded that "there are not lacking elements of the tragic," that "there are some very fine descriptions of the New Zealand bush," and that "there is a common disposition to turn away from New Zealand stories as lacking in novelty and spice, but those who take up *The Toll of the Bush* will not finally lay it aside until the last line has been read."

Actually there is a wide sense of the busy, struggling life of the pioneers in the little river settlements on this remote South Pacific frontier, which gives the novel a memorable solidity and looks forward to later, similar studies such as Jane Mander's *The Story of a New Zealand River* (1920). The book's more personal statement relates to Satchell's sense of being "orphaned" by his voluntary exile to New Zealand and by his father's death after his arrival. His identification with the hero, Geoffrey, is strongly marked—the books in the box, his sense that the old life is dead and gone, his feeling of his inadequacy as a pioneer. It is worth noting here that the Websters and his other Hokianga friends called him "the little duke." Certainly by temperament and education he belonged with the wealthy type of settlers like the Websters, and his affectionate portrait of John Webster as Major Milward is one of the warmer aspects of the novel. Is it possible that Eve Milward, the Major's blonde daughter, was a daughter of John Webster whom Satchell was in love with, and that the novel presents a consummation of this love which did not take place in real life?

Satchell makes good structural use of the bush of his title. It hems the settlers in; it incorporates the hostility of the cosmic power in their struggle against the dominating world of nature; its supernatural force is clearly suggested. Satchell's technical mastery also comes out in the smooth, supple movement of the prose in his descriptions of the great bush fire. Throughout, his sense of language, his use of prose both formal and colloquial, is of a high quality, and his handling of personal relations is subtle and assured.

Whatever its faults, the novel's publication was a literary event of the first importance. It was one of the finest pieces of imaginative writing yet produced in the country. Satchell got right inside his New Zealand material by showing through his hero a sensitive imagination, tuned to European attitudes and responses, trying to cope with the scenes and conditions of the new land in the South Pacific.

He went deeper than in *The Land of the Lost*. Possibly he was influenced by the example of George Eliot, who had seen her own novels as more than social criticism, for like her he tried now to expose and explore genuine moral issues, to investigate areas of spiritual controversy, and look into psychological as well as social problems. *The Toll of the Bush* is supremely a criticism of life as a whole—not just New Zealand life. Yet the freshness of the New Zealand scene, the air of transition from one culture to another, the spirit of pioneering struggles on a frontier, give the novel its special interest.

7   *The Elixir of Life*

By April, 1906, Satchell had sold his splendid house and furniture in Grange Road and moved his family to Hauraki Street, Birkenhead, where rents were cheaper. He had lost his money through unwise or unlucky investments in the third, shortlived, Thames gold-mining boom. In many ways the happiest and most productive era in his life had ended; yet his best work as a novelist was still to come.

About the middle of 1906 he sent his London agent, J. B. Pinker, his old story, "The House on the Headland," which Pinker was unable to sell for him. But his excellent new story, "After His Kind," whose inter-racial theme anticipates the ideas behind *The Greenstone Door*, appeared in *The Red Funnel* on July 1st. Almost a year later, on May 6, 1907, he sent Pinker the script of his third novel, *The Elixir of Life,* which was published immediately by Chapman and Hall but received a poor press.

The Elixir of Life is a medical novel, set in the framework of a sea voyage and shipwreck. The voyage is based on Satchell's own experience of 1886, but the date of events is moved forward twenty years. The book's two heroes are Alan Vincent, a brilliant scientist—a New Zealander returning from study and research in England—and Philip Westland. Vincent is an ambiguous character, while short, slight Westland, whose face indicates "a dual nature," is rather like Satchell himself in his London days, a brooding, mercurial temperament: "From the deepest bottom of pessimism the man's spirit seemed to leap suddenly to the supreme heights of optimism." Through these two Satchell explores new moral and social problems.

Yet the novel does not go deeply enough into either the moral or social questions it raises, to be fully satisfying. It goes a long way, then it stops short; there is a feeling of incompleteness about it. The tone of the writing reaches an unexpected shrillness in places, and there are lapses in the quality of the prose. It resembles *The Last Cruise of the "Wanderer,"* by Satchell's old friend John Webster ("equally a lover of strange scenes and romantic adventures") which describes Benjamin Boyd's voyage from California to Australia with the aim of setting up a social and political organization in the Solomon Islands, where Boyd was killed by the islanders.

But social criticism is only a minor part of Satchell's aim. When his voyagers are wrecked on an island in the South Indian Ocean, the behavior of the community of stranded travellers does give him scope for social satire, and he makes provocative deductions on the question of public leadership. It is the medical side of *The Elixir of Life* which dominates, however, and it is here, almost inevitably, that it is least successful. Neither the idea nor the title was original. Balzac had used the title already, as had Hawthorne in his unfinished *Septimus Felton or the Elixir of Life*. There was also H.G. Wells's rather different novel about a scientist doctor, called *The Island of Doctor Moreau*. But Satchell's handling of the theme is both original and imaginative as far as he goes. His imagination extends itself to new limits here, as well as in new directions.

It is clear from a study of Satchell's private papers that *The Elixir of Life* began as a story of shipboard life, based on notes he had made, but now lost, of his voyage from England to New Zealand in 1886. The *Waima* is the *Arawa* on which he came out; the ports of call on the voyage are the same. He has merely increased the tonnage from 5,200 to 6,500 and changed the name of the ship's owners from Shaw Savill to the New Zealand Shipping Company. The *Arawa* was even detained at Capetown for eighteen hours, just as the fictional ship is held up by an incident that involves the book's hero, Philip Westland. More significant, a passenger on the *Arawa*, John Hickson, died of consumption between Capetown and Hobart, just as Harold Severne dies in the novel.

When exactly the novel of shipboard life grew into the novel about a magical elixir is not clear. As it now stands, the first 190 pages deal with shipboard events, and a further 130 are about happenings on the island. But the idea of the elixir may have come to Satchell in 1902, when on March 15th an anonymous article appeared in the *Graphic* called "Seeking the Elixir of Life." This may have given him some clues if he did not actually write it himself. The article describes the work of Dr Robart of Paris; also of Dr Brown-Sequard, Dr Koch, and Eli Mechnikoff of the Paris Pasteur Institute. Both Dr Koch and the men of the Pasteur Institute are mentioned with some emphasis in the novel. The article gives a historical summary of research on elixirs, noting that Hermes Trismegistus was the first to proclaim that certain medicines would prolong life. It also mentions the work in this direction of Roger Bacon with his serum, and Alphonso, Ponce de Leon.

A year later, on March 28, 1903, an advertisement appeared in the *Graphic* touting Dr James William Kidd of Fort Wayne, Indiana, under this heading: "Marvellous Elixir of Life Discovered by Famous Doctor Scientist That Cures Every Known Ailment . . . The Secret of Long Life of Olden Times Revived." The advertisement was repeated in April. One cannot help wondering if Satchell's doctor-scientist hero in the novel, Dr Alan Vincent, a brilliant young New Zealander, could have been inspired by the advertisement of Dr Kidd.

Whatever the information that led to the novel's genesis, it is plain enough that Satchell fell victim to a common belief of the time in beneficial elixirs, one to which famous medical men lent their support, even if it was also exploited by quacks. The treatment of the elixir theme in the novel is highly idealistic, and every attempt is made by Satchell to give it credibility. But his own private doubts come out in the ambiguous nature of his portrait of his scientist hero, Dr Alan Vincent, and his behavior after the elixir is found.

8   *The Greenstone Door*

Despite Satchell's comparative poverty now, home life continued smoothly at Hauraki Street in the tranquility of the North Shore. His growing family were happy and healthy. He quietly cultivated a splendid flower garden and a beautiful fernery. All his talents as a family man were nourished by his young children. He built them a puppet theatre with twenty-four dolls, took photographs for their special entertainment with homemade cameras, taught them German student songs, made for them a large collection of moths and butterflies, and built two aviaries containing three hundred Australian birds.

James B. Pinker wrote on July 21, 1908, that he had sold to the *National Review* Satchell's article on "New Zealand and the Emigrants." But Satchell's real interest was currently in the theater. In August, Kaber Harrison Danbury of Onehunga read two plays he had written, with a view to production. In October, Pinker sold "The Sun Girl" (probably his old story "Te Kotiro Ma") to the *Grand Magazine.* In April, 1909, J.C. Williamson's in Sydney read but did not produce his play *The Divided Note.* Pinker sold "The Deserters" to the *Lady's Realm,* but could not place "A Sense of Humour," "The Right of Way," or "Herr Lieber's Melons."

During the same year Satchell became secretary of the Auckland Horticultural Society, holding this part time job for ten years. In June, 1910, the family made another move, this time to Church Street, Northcote (also on the North Shore). Here Satchell began work on his last novel, *The Greenstone Door,* in which the trend of his imagination toward the dark, shadowy, guilty side of life—toward the romantic and the fantastic— received full expression.

The novel was long considered and carefully planned. He first tried to locate the temporary quarters occupied by Sir George Grey in 1848 after Government House was burnt down, by writing to the Brown family, and to Sir John Logan Campbell, who said it was the house called St. Kevens in Karangahape

Road. This house was to be the setting for important early scenes in the novel, which were contrasted with the primitive yet idyllic life of the remote bush pa where his new hero was to grow up. As further preparation for the book, Satchell walked through the steep, bush-clad Waipa and Waikato country where the most moving events of the novel are laid.

In 1911, his ninth child, Rosalind, was born at Northcote. Shortly afterward he made another move, to Onewa Road, Birkenhead. Here he rented an old, colonial-style house big enough for the eleven members of the family, who were now joind by a twelfth, his cousin Frank Tomlinson. With the house there were five acres of land, mostly orchard. Half of the orchard was wired off with netting and a large poultry farm was established by the two men as a joint venture.

During the Auckland Industrial, Agricultural and Mining Exhibition of 1912-13, Satchell with H.T. Goldie and N.R.W. Thomas ran the horticultural section in what is now the Winter Garden of the Auckland Domain. This work reflected his life-long interest in flowers. He exhibited his own chrysanthemums and won several prizes. He also did a number of oil paintings at this time, though there is some doubt, unfortunately for our own curiosity, whether these still exist.

His new novel dealt with the growing-up of a boy in Maori territory during the 1840s and '50s, and his coming to manhood in the Maori Wars of the '60s. It was completed in 1914 and published in July—in London by Sidgwick and Jackson and in New York by the Macmillan Co. However, it appears to have aroused little excitement among reviewers. The *Athenaeum* of July 18th merely said it was "a readable story of adventure" in which "the characters both English and Maori are well drawn." One reader who did enjoy it was Colonel H. Stratton Bates, former official Interpreter to Sir George Grey and General Cameron during the Taranaki and Waikato wars, who was "able to recognise the excellence of your sketch of the Maori customs and modes of expression" and considered the portrait of Grey in the book to be "lifelike."

Although the usual reason given for the failure of *The Greenstone Door* in 1914 is that no one was interested in an old colonial war when a new European war was just beginning, the book's strong anti-war tone was another reason. Its tragic hero,

Purcell, the white trader living among the Maoris, who rears
the boy Cedric Tregarthen and sides with the Maoris against
the British, actually renounces his British citizenship and de-
nounces the evils of patriotism. These sentiments were repugnant to British readers in 1914. Out in New Zealand a strong
sympathy for the British fight against the Germans was causing
an upsurge of patriotism—in the same way as it had in the Boer
War—in which Satchell himself fervently took part by writing
a series of newspaper articles.

No one at this time could accept such of Purcell's anti-war
statements as:

Patriotism in a civilised state surrounded by barbarians is doubtless
a virtue of the finest; but the patriotism that, as in Europe, keeps a
number of civilised communities at arm's length or incites them to
the destruction of one another is surely none but the reverse. . . .
From the point of view of the patriot I am doubtless a monster, but
considered as merely a human being it may be that I have my redeeming points.

This fundamental truth, which was unacceptable in 1914, shows
how far Satchell's thinking had progressed, and is a key to the
new quality and universal depth of the book.

But why did Satchell turn back to the period of the Maori
Wars for the setting of his last novel? Why for instance did he
never write about contemporary life in the "little city" of Auckland where he lived for forty years? This question is crucial to
an understanding of his vision as an artist and his strengths
and limitations as a novelist. On the other hand, if he wanted to
be historical, the experiences of men like John Webster in early
Hokianga had contained enough material for a dozen novels. In
creating the figure of Purcell he had certainly drawn upon the
career of his wife's grandfather, Joseph Bryers, who had lived
with the Maoris in the 1830s (before New Zealand became a
British colony) in "the days when the white man came alone
into the native settlement and picked his wife from the bright-
eyed kotiros of the hapu."

However, the war against the Waikato confederation of tribes
in the 1860s, when they crowned their own king to set up
against the British queen, was the central action which focussed

the whole era of conflict between the British and Maori civilizations in early New Zealand. It was this basic clash which Satchell was most deeply concerned with as an artist. There is undoubtedly a greater sense of urgency, a feeling of disaster and tragedy pervading the book, which shows his own anxiety not only about race relations in his contemporary world, but about the whole problem of people living together everywhere—about human society generally.

Again in a sensitive way Satchell identifies himself with his orphaned hero Cedric. The personality of Purcell incorporates many features of Satchell's dead father. Purcell's role as educator and foster-father of Cedric is challenged by another father-figure, Sir George Grey, for whom Cedric works as private secretary. Many incidents in the book point back to experiences in Satchell's London life after his return from Heidelberg. Thus not only is Cedric in love with the heroine, Helenora; he also acts as her tutor and spends some time teaching her German. They read together in German Schiller's poem, "The Bell". They also read Wordsworth together.

The German elements in the book would combine with its anti-war tone to make it unpopular with readers in 1914. The author's modern sense of *angst,* concealed beneath the story's romantic surface, was bound to be unappreciated then, as was his pleading the cause of humanity and tolerance above racial conflict. Many did not see then in this novel the great compassion, or the beauty and mystery of a universal work of art.

Satchell was now, however, involved in New Zealand's disastrous part in World War I, in which New Zealand deaths in the fighting were greater than those of Belgium, a battlezone country with six times New Zealand's population. Three of Satchell's sons, Tom, Allan, and William, fought in France and Palestine, and luckily all survived. During these years Satchell wrote a number of weekly columns of a somewhat meditative nature about the war in the *New Zealand Herald.*

In 1917 he finally left Onewa Road, to live in Havelock Street, Birkenhead. At the same time he obtained a job as accountant for the Stanley P. Gibbons Timber Company at Kopu, about four miles from Thames—a Mr Gibbons had been manager of the old Webster brothers' sawmill on the Hokianga. He went home by boat to Auckland once a fortnight, until a house became available at Kopu, when all the family moved there. He stayed at Kopu for eleven years, disappointed at the failure of *The Greenstone Door* and suffering from stomach ulcers. In 1928 he wrote a children's story, *The Book of Joso,* and returned to Auckland to live in Malvern Road, Morningside, working in the Swanson Street offices of the company until it went out of business in 1936. In 1932 he moved to his final home at 37 Queensway, Mount Roskill.

His last years were brightened by a revival of interest in *The Greenstone Door.* An unknown young musician had written him a remarkable tribute:

To read *The Greenstone Door* is an epoch in one's life and the occasion for deepest interest and keenest delight. Naturally the book is NOT forgotten and never will be. None of the great classics in music, art and literature ever could be. New Zealand and New Zealanders owe more to you than they can ever repay, and readers from the other side of the world are indebted to you for bringing something very big and lasting into their lives.[6]

Other readers expressed similar feelings, and many who read the book even today have the same kind of reaction to it. In the 1930s a small group of admirers in Auckland began to work for republication. *The Greenstone Door* had started to live again in obedience to the general law that the highest art is not as a rule the big popular success of its day but by its subtle influence on a discerning few, creates in time its own audience through strong identity of feeling. It was reprinted in 1935 and has since gone through many editions and become a guide and inspiration for many present-day New Zealand novelists.

Satchell's old age was saddened, however, by Susan's death in 1937. She had been a loyal wife and outstanding mother, silent and stoical and enduring all that marriage to a man like Satchell meant. Her image flickers briefly but strongly in the pages of his books, in devoted, warm-hearted characters such as Roma, Puhi-Huia, Meri, and even the strange, unnamed "girl nobody want" of the short story "E Kotiro Ma" and the beautiful, lustrous-eyed Mallow sisters of *The Toll of the Bush.*

In 1938 Satchell's son William and family moved into the house to look after him. All nine children eventually married and raised their own families, so that he became at the end a kind of genial patriarch. The same year saw *The Land of the Lost* reprinted. He earned little from the royalties of his books, but made some money by accountancy and auditing jobs, augmented in 1939 by a Civil List pension in recognition of his work as a novelist. Satchell was then only the third New Zealander to receive such an award from the government.

At the last his son George cared for him also, and he continued vigorous till the end. He died in a Princes Street private hospital on October 21, 1942, aged 82. New Zealand newspapers published tributes, and the Sydney *Bulletin* did not forget its distinguished old contributor: under the heading "A Maoriland Novelist," the *Bulletin* said he was one of New Zealand's best novelists, "if not with his *The Greenstone Door* the very best." He would have enjoyed reading those words.

CHAPTER 2

The Beauty of Life: Stories and Poems

ANY critical analysis of Satchell's art must begin with his short stories. His output in the field of short fiction is not large; there are less than forty tales, sketches, and stories which can definitely be identified as his. Yet they are more than an addendum to his novels: they are their forerunners in themes and treatment. They increase our understanding of his novels because they reveal in smaller scale the topics and types of human behavior that obsessed him. They illuminate the darkness surrounding his great subjects, by showing his first tentative handling of his dominant ideas. They also display the early development of his prose style.

The short story form of writing is well suited to life on the frontiers of civilization. Satchell wrote mainly about the pioneers, but unexpectedly his stories are not consistently concerned with New Zealand's early racial theme, which absorbed the interest of his contemporaries. A. A. Grace's *Maoriland Stories,* which came out in 1895, soon followed by his better known *Tales of a Dying Race* (1901), and William Baucke's *Where the White Man Treads* (1905), were stories about old Maoris in their decadence, before the modern Maori revival began. No doubt there was something romantic then about the supposedly dying race, which attracted the art of Grace and Baucke. Satchell, however, had a very different attitude when he came to write his fiction, despite his remarks to Allan Fea in the letter posted after his arrival in New Zealand in 1886. He did not in fact deal fully with the racial theme until his last short story, "After His Kind".

Satchell's English stories in *Will o' the Wisp* are not nearly so bad as their neglect by modern readers might suggest. They certainly did not deserve the condemnation of the *Academy* reviewer in 1883. The best of the collection (it makes play with

[53]

a flickering lantern held in the hand of the hero, young Eyton)
is the first story, "The Black Mirror," which is a supernatural,
morbid romance about an ancient castle by the sea, a dying family, and an ancestral curse, almost worthy of the great E. T. A.
Hoffmann himself.

Some idea of the style of these stories can be judged from the
opening sentence of "The Black Mirror":

As night advanced the wind, that had been blowing a perfect hur-
ricane across the wild grey sea—almost threatening at times to blow
me from my foothold upon the brown slippery rocks, and hurl me
headlong down the precipitous cliff—died gradually away to a low
moaning sound.[1]

This gothic note is repeated in "The Black Banner and the
Scarlet Flag," a less successful story about another castle and
a wife's murder of her husband's lover.

A short supernatural tale is "The Sisters of the Dusty Grange,"
in which the narrator and his artist friend, on a walking tour
through England, come upon an old brick mansion and meet
some curious ghosts. "Lemuel Legarde," a tale of a miscarriage
of justice in France in 1838, is a kind of horror story very typical of the period, and like all these tales it shows the violent
activity of a lively imagination. The last in the book, "The Mystery of Comberton Hall," is a more detailed venture into the
feudal past, spread over several generations, and with all the
creaking machinery of the pseudosupernatural which marks the
gothic phase in English fiction.

Although Satchell's style of writing changed greatly after his
break with England and his exposure to the fresh New Zealand
environment, the mannerisms of German Romanticism did not
completely disappear. It is possible to see a return to the pattern
of the *Will o' the Wisp* tales, handled in a more sophisticated
way, in several places in his later fiction.

1   The Great Unemployed Scheme

Satchell's first identifiable publication as a New Zealand writer,
"The Great Unemployed Scheme," shows a satirical treatment
quite different from his English tales. It is a piece of boisterous,
sustained irony, not absolutely certain in tone, and containing

some rough writing. But its importance lies in its attempt to deal with the actuality of life after the fantastic nature of the *Will o' the Wisp* stories. Its bitter realism emphasises the interval of eleven years between his English and New Zealand work.

The central character of "The Great Unemployed Scheme" is Plumley Sarks, an Auckland inventor, who after inventing a machine for shuffling cards and dealing them, and a robot typewriter for taking down speeches in Parliament, thinks up a scheme for dealing with the colony's large number of unemployed workers. Sarks sells his idea to the Prime Minister in Wellington, and soon the nation's economy miraculously recovers its stability. But when the Minister of Lands for New South Wales in Australia is attracted to New Zealand to inspect the scheme, and mysteriously disappears, a public inquiry reveals that the unemployed workers have also physically vanished. A cynical explanation is made by a government spokesman:

We selected a spot remote as possible from civilisation, wild, bush-clad, presenting well-nigh insuperable obstacles to the settler, and there we turned our men loose with their wives and families, tools and a certain quantity of provisions . . . their sections were pegged and there they were left.

Unfortunately, no word has been heard from them since. Torrential rains have washed out all roads, and the settlers are presumed to have died of starvation in the bush.

That this situation was not too great a travesty of the actual conditions under which Satchell himself worked and lived in Hokianga County is fairly evident. And although as fiction "The Great Unemployed Scheme" is something of a tall yarn, its maturity and urbanity show how much Satchell had developed as an artist. The cynicism and heartlessness of the "inventor," and the hypocrisy of the nation's parliamentarians, are qualities completely absent from his early work. Yet the sharpness of his feelings, and the savagery of his attack on the social scheme of things, are concealed by a bantering note and a matter-of-factness of exposition.

The two linked short stories, "Why I Came to New Zealand" and "Emotions of an Emigrant," show Satchell groping further in his art toward an understanding of New Zealand scenes and attitudes. They describe in comic fashion the way in which a new-chum settler spends a night lost and alone in eerie, rugged North Auckland bush country. They contain some good writing, such as the following account of the lost traveller's discovery of a waterfall in the dense bush.

> The water came down a cleft of the mountain, like a huge, slithery, silver panther, to slip away out of sight among the ferns at the foot of the hill... Above, the thickets were black as midnight, so that the cataract pouring forth from their midst and taking of a sudden the full splendour of the moon-light seemed less of water than of fire, less inanimate than a living presence. The ground about me was more or less clear of vegetation. A solitary tree-fern stood in the full brilliance of the moon at the foot of the fall, trembling incessantly to the ponderous impact of the descending stream, and looking like a startled and dishevelled Naiad whose remote solitude had been suddenly visited by the glowing presence of a God.[2]

The controlled handling of words and the formal periods of the prose in such a passage, unique in New Zealand fiction at this time, were an important contribution to Satchell's art as a novelist in his best work later on.

A sense of the New Zealand past becomes apparent for the first time in "From a Northern Gumfield." Here the regional quality of Satchell's fiction is more marked also. If Satchell wanted to create his own fictional world, "From a Northern Gumfield" is one of his best introductions to it. It is brief, concise, and pointed, with a characteristic romantic touch like the tint of a watercolor overlying his realistic details of everyday life.

The opening paragraph has a dry, sardonic, essay-like quality often found in his prose. He contrasts the great Hokianga kauri forests with "the bleak, scrub-covered lands" where now "the gum-digger labours at his task," yet which "in the olden days were shadowed by woods as fine as any now standing." On the rich and extensive field of Kawerua on the West Coast two young gumdiggers, Joe and Jack, are packing their swags after two years of hard work. As they canter along the beach to the

Hokianga Heads they discuss the money they have earned from the sale of their gum. Jack proposes to use his money to get married to Margaret, a settler's daughter on the Kohu Kohu, and his reunion with her forms the climax of the tale.

The strong, easy-flowing language is as well controlled as before, but the story contains a new mood for Satchell. In spite of the tartness of the opening paragraph there is a depth of contentment, compassion and love—a sense of the beauty of life. The writing is that of a man who has for the first time discovered his power and recognized his real themes and his task. "The cool breeze which renders the New Zealand summer night so sweet and invigorating already blew gently in from the sea." "By this time the moon had risen in the sky and poured her soft light on the golden sandhills and the broad river." Such peaceful notes as these are unusual in the prevailing ironic mode of his work. The story has warmth and emotional richness.

On the other hand his sense of evil as a cosmic, supernatural force—possessing a vitality beyond human control, and capable of destroying human life—is evident in "The Man Who Went North." This story shows Satchell's awareness of the evil inherent in the barbarisms and cruelties of ancient Maori life as practiced in the rites of the tohungas or priests—an awareness that becomes so powerful a part of the effect in *The Greenstone Door*. The story is clearly based on an experience of John Webster in the early days when he accidentally discovered some Maori burial caves at Horeke, while out pig-hunting near his brother William's sawmill. Webster described the incident many years later in his *Reminiscences of an Old Settler,* and emphasized the atmosphere of tapu [taboo] at the caves.

The hero of the story, Desmond, a student of burial customs throughout the world, visits a Maori village northwest of Russell with his wife Margaret. There is authentic description of the settlement and of the ancient, nearly blind "medicine man or tohunga" who says on hearing of Desmond's quest: "Friend, you are to go north." When in a cave beneath a rock near a waterfall he finds the embalmed body of "a great and renowned chief" this closely agrees with Webster's account. But the description of the two embalmed warriors crouched at his knees with their faces hidden, tattooed and naked except for loincloths, and the way Margaret, following the direction of the "pointing shrivelled finger" of the chief, falls to her death in a pit forty feet deep and full of skeletons, show a return in Satchell's writing to the old gothic note.

The same awareness of evil and horror is given lighter treatment in "An Author's Model," a more conventional story. In "The Yellow Dwarf: A Tale of a Mine" he introduces one of his favorite motifs—already hinted at in "From a Northern Gumfield" —the attempted thwarting of the hero's love for his betrothed through the usually unscrupulous efforts of a rival lover. The setting is the Thames goldfields, and the mine's owner, Mark Weatherly, is like many of Satchell's heroes, an English immigrant recently arrived in New Zealand. The story tells how Weatherly discovers the lost reef of gold in the mine after he has been knocked down and left to die by his rival in love named Sendall. However, the writing lacks distinction and there is little real feeling in it.

He returns to his North Auckland locale in "A Martyr to Circumstantial Evidence," based on his experiences as a storekeeper. The setting is Rawene township. When the store is robbed of five cases of re-scraped, clear gum, the cash from the till, and all the trading records (including £1500 of unpaid bills), a local shoemaker named George Barker is convicted of the burglary and sent to prison. But afterwards the villagers believe they have made a mistake and that Barker is innocent. The colony's governor is petitioned, a committee is formed, and Barker is released. The prime mover in this act is the local clergyman, Mr. Milmouse, who accuses Bagstock, a local wharfman, of having committed the crime.

Bagstock is the story's martyr. "The wharfman by this time led the life of a pariah ... Except on the day of the steamer's visit he rarely left the tumble-down shanty on the beach." Local larrikins throw stones at him. Mr. Milmouse visits him daily to ask him to repent. "His appearance became rapidly more disreputable, his body thinner, his face more hatchet-like." Because of the townspeople's suspicion he can get no work. He eventually dies of starvation.

On his deathbed he says to Mr. Milmouse: "I reckon it's the confession you're after and I'd better own up and have done with it." When the parson asks him where he has hidden the store's debtors' books, he replies: "I burnt them! I burnt them!

I burnt them! There! Does that satisfy you?" [3] Thus Bagstock is the first crude portrait of many social outcasts in Satchell's fiction. As for poor blind foolish Mr Milmouse, as he "tucked 'this our brother' reverently away in the cemetery" he did not know what a sin he had committed against mankind, even though the reader has long since realized that Bagstock is innocent.

It is Satchell's compassionate tenderness for the martyred wharfman which gives the story its fascination, despite some misplaced facetiousness which was his concession to his newspaper readers. Again and again it is upon such men that Satchell focuses his inventiveness. He was fascinated by the destitute, by life's victims—"the lost" of his first novel's title.

2 *The Maorilander Speaks*

Of the many short stories included in the seven weekly issues of Satchell's literary magazine *The Maorilander,* only three or four need be considered seriously. There is little of interest in "The Stone Stable Mystery," his pedestrian attempt to write a detective story, nor is there much worth while in some of the shorter sketches and anecdotes in the magazine.

The theme of the social outcast emerges again in "The Babes in the Bush." This story portrays the thoughts and emotions of Daniel Drinkwood, a red-headed fugitive convict from the settlements across the Tasman Sea, who is hiding in a *nikau* hut in a remote bush gully near Hokianga Heads. He is on the lookout for a ship, *The Flying Hope,* whose captain has promised to take him to Sydney. He sees two children—they belong to the local constable, Mr. Garland—who are lost in the bush near his hideout. They are a girl of five or six and a boy of three or four, and the boy is close to death. Drinkwood brings them to his hut for shelter, and although he is close to starvation himself he shares his last food with them. Finally, while trying to guide a party of rescuers to the lost children, he becomes trapped in a supplejack thicket and dies.

Drinkwood is presented with sympathy. The story is quietly told, without sentimentality. The children, for instance, dislike Drinkwood. "His self-sacrifice, his awkward yet evident friendliness, his unwavering patience and dog-like humility, were alike powerless to disarm the enmity of his small companions." The

basic humanity of even this pathetic reject of society is emphasized: "The mind of the criminal was occupied with dim
thoughts, the shadowy outlines of vast ideas." It should be noted
too that the incident of the supplejacks is used with greater
dramatic force in *The Toll of the Bush.*

Among the comic sketches in *The Maorilander* is "The Stiff
'Un," a horseracing yarn about a horse named Cyclone, its ir-
repressible jockey Tom Welch, and an Englishman named Westwood, who "had come out to the colony for the sale of his
health." It is a typical racetrack yarn about jiggery-pokery
[trickery] with the horses, distinctive for being told in the vernacular. Another comic story, "Wilkes' Sanatorium," is somewhat
in the O. Henry tradition. It describes a confidence trick played
by Wilkes on the gullible people who visit his sanatorium on the
site of an abandoned gold mine near Thames, where the healing
soda springs and sulphur baths are all fakes. Much of the charm
of the story comes from the narrator's viewpoint—he is a Mr.
White, formerly Wilkes' partner at the mine.

Quite a different vein is exposed in "Te Kotiro Ma" (The
White Girl) in which Harold Templar, again a typical Satchell
narrator (the Englishman recently arrived in New Zealand), discovers a white girl "in the garb of a Maori." She is hoeing a
plantation of potatoes and corn at a North Auckland Maori settlement. Templar is attracted by her blue eyes and her hair, yellow like ripe corn, which "rolled and rippled to her hips." When
Templar asks her name she replies in broken English.

"The girl nobody want—the girl leave behind. . . . The Maori no
leave—he keep all the time."
"Are you satisfied—happy? . . . Would you like to have friends of
your own blood? To see the sights of the world, the cities, the people;
to dress in beautiful clothes?"

Templar meets her again after dark in the trees, and plans to
elope with her on the following night. But next day a telegram
arrives announcing his succession to a baronetcy and requiring
his presence in England. This situation is rather like that of
Cedric Tregarthen and Puhi-Huia in *The Greenstone Door,* but
the ending is different.

Satchell wrote later about a young man and a real Maori girl in "After His Kind." This key story in his art, written after he had published his two novels of pioneering life, can be analyzed here because of its commitment to a multi-racial view of society. Thus in his handling of the racial theme Satchell differs from writers like Grace and Baucke, who saw a "dying race"—differs even from a novelist like Harry B. Vogel in his *A Maori Maid* (1898). He was too deeply and personally involved to be a detached observer; he could see a new society emerging.

In "After His Kind" he has moved from the presentation of a white pioneering community to a glimpse of the marriage of a white man and a Maori girl, showing how the mingling of the two races was in actual fact coming about. He sees as if in a vision the strong, handsome, upright young sons of the future, when the story's hero, Merton, goes against the traditions of "his kind" by choosing a Maori wife instead of the beautiful but cold white girl he was expected to marry. So by that reversal or twist which is characteristic of Satchell's best stories, the reader discovers that "his kind" is really mankind.

In the story's cleverly-written dream sequence Satchell shows Merton visualizing how dull life with the shallow society girl in Auckland would be by contrast with what the Maori girl had to offer. But to begin with, the story's small-town setting (Rawene again) is described with boldness and economy of narrative outlay. Merton is the storekeeper, and he tells the Maori girl, Meri, that he can't marry her because she is only fifteen. She has the perfect answer to this quibbling:

"Some girl eleven. Plenty—*plenty* girl only fourteen. . . . Judge Dalton's wife only Maori girl, same as me. . . . I not a poor girl. Plenty land here, plenty up te river—all over. My father te big chief." [4]

When Merton goes to church in the old school hall to hear a sermon by the English missionary who is making his annual visit to Hokianga, he sees his near-betrothed, Mildred McGregor, a settler's daughter who wants him to take her to Auckland, as an already fading, colorless lily, in contrast with Meri's glowing tropical radiance like "an hibiscus newly opened to the sun." The triteness of the simile is an indication of the dubious quality of the feeling. But although Meri scarcely exists as a person, she is a sketch of something innocent and good, a foretaste of the more fully portrayed Maori and halfcaste women of *The Green-stone Door:* Roma, Puhi-Huia, and Pepepe.

A story of 1904, "The Divided Note," is mainly interesting for its use in the theme of two brothers in love with the same woman, and for its experimental style of writing, which approximates that of a stage play. The setting is North Auckland again. Part I, "The Dead Man in the Sands," takes place on the beach, and the protagonists, Billy Jones, a Cockney gumdigger, and the sinister Doctor, discuss the recent death in a sandstorm of their consumptive gumdigger mate whom they know as Briggs. Part II, "The Girl of the Cliffs," introduces Mr. Haslett, the scientist (who has come north to see the migration of the godwits or kuaka on their annual journey to Siberia from New Zealand) and Winnifred Marsden. Part III, "The House on the Headland," introduces Horace Marsden, an English exile, once a Senior Wrangler [teacher] at a famous English college, who has been in New Zealand for fifteen years, and his wife. The plot hinges on the discovery of the torn half of a £10,000 banknote in the pocket of the dead man, Briggs, of which Marsden possesses the other half. The money is an inheritance, and Briggs is really Horace Marsden's brother Edward. Both men were in love with Horace's wife in the old days before his marriage.

This somewhat morbid triangle of an unhappy love affair is forgotten in Part IV, "The Migration of the Godwits," when the long-awaited flight is watched by Haslett and Winnifred, by "a bare ridge of sand; a waste of storm-tossed waters, grey and red in the light of the setting sun." The migration is "one of the wonders of the world." As the birds fly "higher still into the clear cold altitudes that lifted them above the petty considerations of earthly inequalities," a new love affair is seen to be springing up between the young couple which will be more fruitful than the dark, unhappy English past of the older people up at the house. The flight of the godwits is interpreted as a sign of the freedom and beauty of life in New Zealand; and Haslett, the man of science, is going to enjoy that freedom with Winnifred. It is a romantic setting, a new world atmosphere, as Winnifred is aware when she says to Haslett, who gazes with a kind of ecstasy at the thousands of migrating birds: "And you claimed you were not romantic." Brooding at the house, her father is freed by his brother's death, yet has nothing left in life but the two torn halves of the £10,000 banknote. The story is not fully worked out; in particular the role of Mrs. Marsden, the dead man's old lover, is not fully explained. But the general tone and feeling of the story are prophetic of Satchell at his best.

3 *The Racial Delusion*

Between 1894 and 1918 Satchell wrote thirty or so short essays on various topics, the first of which was "A Football Match" in the *Graphic*. His handling of the short essay was assured, and it might be said that in gaining a novelist in Satchell, New Zealand lost an essayist. He expresses many of his ideas more directly in these essays than in his fiction. Thus he discusses the possibility of life on other planets in "Things in Heaven and Earth," suggesting with mock seriousness that the moon is inhabited by a race of beings endowed with "all but supernatural sagacity" who live hidden in its interior. We on earth are poor descendants of the moonites, less brilliant, physically and spiritually changed by earth's living conditions. This idea was developed further in "Interplanetary Communication."

Reflections on war, which form a large part of this aspect of Satchell's work, begin with an essay called "Laughing War Off the Face of the Earth." Here he suggests that, "perhaps the time is coming when the civilized races will be unable to wage war, owing to the refusal of their troops to regard the matter seriously"—a thought which anticipates his attack on patriotism in *The Greenstone Door*. His later writings about war, published after that novel, reveal him at times as painfully jingoistic, as though he were whipping up newspaper support for an unpopular cause. In one essay called "Afterwards" he presents the theory that "everything that tends to make war more uncertain in its issue, or to increase its horror or its magnitude, must also tend to make it rarer." What would he think of the H-bomb?

His concern that civilization should survive was a deep one. In "The Dream City" he makes a plea for civilization to go on in its present course despite the cataclysm of war, since "every nation is a hucksterer and almost every individual." In "The Man of Destiny" he says: "I am a democrat of democrats"; in "Afterwards" he adds that he wants to see the nations of the world "blossom in liberty under the sun of liberty."

His essay "The Racial Delusion" scoffs at the "Aryans," who even then were raising their wild theories: "There is much loose talk of pure blood." He believes that "every great race is a mixed race, and there is good evidence in support of the theory that the greater the mixture the greater the race. In the United States of America mankind is really undertaking the most colossal of experiments." [5]

Frequently Satchell's thinking anticipates later ideas, and always he takes the most universal view of things—his concern is primarily for mankind in general and the human predicament. He was not just a New Zealander: he was also a citizen of the world. This breadth of view is a source of greatness in his work.

4 *Ballads of War and Peace*

In his best poems Satchell is a story-teller; his talent was a narrative rather than a lyrical one. His interest in the ballad form was a product of this tendency, from the very early *Bedlam Ballads* to the better-known "The Ballad of Stuttering Jim." The *Bedlam Ballads* are juvenilia, but the ballads in the *Will o' the Wisp* collection are more interesting, even though individuality of expression is smothered by strong echoes of the poets he was imitating, such as Sir Walter Scott and Thomas Hood. Hood's method is most obtrusive in "The Lay of the Silver Bells" and "Night," both in the minor tradition of English literary romanticism and marred by poor writing: "Sadly the wind was sobbing in the trees." The title poem is the best. It tells of the marriage of Will o' the Wood and Rose o' the Glen.

> He rode to the gravedigger's open door,
> Where red lay the light on the whitened floor.
> "I pray you, good man, for a golden dower,
> To ring all the bells in the grey church tower,
> When gold gleams the sun, and the day is good;
> Tomorrow's the wedding," quoth Will o' the Wood.

This stanza, in its immaturity and triteness of language, is typical of Satchell's work before he left England. "The Ballad of the Lady Maud" is an attempt to write a border ballad, and "The Enchantress" has a romantic Baltic setting.

The Boer War ballads in the *Patriotic* collection are strident and hark back to the English viewpoint of his youth. Thus the "patriotism" of "Mafeking" is actually "For the honour and glory of England as long as a man may live." "The Hour and the Man" speaks fervently of "the pride of the Empire of half the world and the pride of the Empire's flag." A third poem of similar style was called "The Might of England." He reached his worst depths of banality in "The Uitlander and the Empire," which describes how the British pioneer settler "has battered out the way / With the bullet and the bottle and the Book." The pioneer has not only, he says, spread the British empire over "half the continents of earth," he has also "taught the coloured cannibal to sing 'God Save the Queen'— / A song that coloured cannibals adore." All the poems in this group might have been written by a man totally opposed to the William Satchell who wrote *The Greenstone Door,* and the most charitable explanation of them is that they were written to make quick money when he was over-excited by events of the war.

A more genuine expression of feeling comes in "Europe and Co," a poem which attacks colonialism and the empire-building policies of 1900. He looks forward to present-day attitudes in his warning to the European countries that they "can't go on forever redistributing the earth." A time will come, he says, when they will find that "black and white are very much the same." As far as colonialism is concerned, "You will have to keep progressing till you've learnt from facts distressing / That it isn't all a money-making game." In another poem, "The English at the Gates of Pretoria," he reminds his readers that just as the bright flame of imperial Rome died, so will the British empire perish.

In the remainder of the *Patriotic* volume Satchell makes a genuine attempt to present an individual poetic vision of New Zealand life. There is a boisterous bush ballad called "Song of the Gumfield," extracts from which were later inserted into the text of his first novel. The poem describes conditions in the great depression of the 'Eighties when the North Auckland gumfields were a dubious sanctuary for the unemployed, the deadbeats, and the remittance men who drifted out from the cities to "the slighted, blighted North, where the giant kauris grow / And the earth is bare and barren."

Like the bush ballads of Henry Lawson, Banjo Paterson, and other Australians, "The Ballad of Stuttering Jim" was written in the form of a campfire yarn, told by Jim himself.

> There was me, and Pell, and Carroty Joe, and
>   Bandy Gray . . .
> And the fire grew dim, and the pipes went out,
>   and the whisky bottle was dry.

Jim, incidentally, doesn't stutter when telling his story, so the exact origin of the title remains a mystery. But the poem reflects the egalitarian democracy of frontier life, where all men whatever their antecedents were treated as equals. It describes in racy rhythms the conflict over a girl between two men—Jim, a local stockhand, and an unnamed remittance man from England.

> For there came a chap to her father's farm, a bit of
>   a ne-er-do-well,
> Who had gone the pace for all it was worth till they
>   shipped him away to hell.

Now the girl is a typical settler's daughter of those days: "She could ride all day, and dance all night, and be up with the morning dew"; but soon Jim found himself cut out by the ne'er-do-well. Yet although she "loved the other chap best," she obeyed the laws of her community and "stuck fast to her plighted troth," that is, to Jim, until one afternoon when she and Jim get lost in the trackless bush and the remittance man comes to their rescue.

Soon all three are lost. The Englishman shares his food with Jim and the girl, until on the sixth day they have nothing left to eat. They light a fire and wait for rescue, drinking water from a swamp and chewing taraire berries. Now Jim commits the unforgiveable frontier sin of keeping to himself some bread which enables him to survive while the other two die of starvation—but not before the girl discovers his treachery and proclaims her true love for the Englishman. The theme of the balladeer living a lifetime of guilt while the pure, noble lovers go to their deaths is a commonplace of ballad literature, but the effect of this poem is qualified by its sometimes labored syntax and forced rhythms. Yet its freshness, bounce, and authenticity make it the best of the collection.

A more ambitious and stylized poem is "Ode to the Vanishing Forests of New Zealand," a conventional and sometimes clumsy attempt to mourn the destruction of much of the New Zealand bush by settlers who were hacking out new farms and homesteads and burning off great tracts of standing timber. Again the effect is spoiled by archaic diction and sentimental references to "kowhai lamps" and "the pensive rimu" and the "rata rude" or "the filmy ferns." The theme of the vanishing forests was a favorite one of poets of the period; it was handled much better, for instance, by William Pember Reeves, whose poetry was recently examined by Keith Sinclair in *William Pember Reeves: New Zealand Fabian* (1965). The impression conveyed is that Satchell had not yet absorbed the scenery of New Zealand into his imagination, a defect which he overcame in his novels, but which stands out in other lyrics in this collection such as "Bellbirds" and "Hinemoa's Song."

The anti-scientific poems are evidence of his resistance to any theory or scheme of life which denies the essential humanity of man. For instance these lines:

> For I am a scientific man
>   Of the Nineteenth Century.
> I put no faith in the tales of old
>   That bygone men believed,
> For it's perfectly plain to a clearer brain
>   That they were all deceived.
> I cut with a knife the beauty of life
>   For I know it is all a dream . . .

The sharpness of the satire, which fixes here on the phrase "the beauty of life," contains a feeling common in Satchell that modern civilization and modern science are destroying too much beauty. As he says in "A Scientific Sing-song": "it makes you feel uncommonly small / To think you're mechanical after all . . . governed despotical, slightly erotical / Penny-in-slotical toys." His attack on the influential mechanical-scientific theories of the time does not conceal the fact that he is a poet of minor ability. Much of what he wrote is forced and artificial, but some of his ballads will continue to be read.

CHAPTER 3

The Hokianga Novels

THERE were many young Englishmen in early New Zealand like the ne'er-do-well hero of "The Ballad of Stuttering Jim," who "had gone the pace for all it was worth till they shipped him away to hell." Some were alcoholics from aristocratic families, who were paid a regular remittance by mail on the condition that they didn't return to England. In *The Land of the Lost,* "hell" was the desolate region east of Taheke in Hokianga County, the largest open gumfield in the district. Here the spokesman of "the lost" is the drunken remittance man Sir Charles Medway, who calls himself Higgins but is known as Bart—the formal abbreviation for Baronet turned into a nickname by the gumdiggers.

At his first appearance Bart emerges from the "dead-house" of the bush pub called the "Scarlet Man," having just recovered from his latest bout of drinking, to meet the hero of the novel, Hugh Clifford, at the dining table. Clifford sees a dishevelled-looking creature of about thirty-five, dressed in the ordinary rough clothing of the digger. His hair is long and unkempt and there is a week's growth of stubble on his chin. His features are clear-cut and aquiline, and might originally have been termed refined, but there is a bloated look about his cheeks and around his bloodshot eyes. He represents the dark, tragic side of pioneer life.

Bart receives Satchell's special compassion, through a creative imagination richly stimulated in describing the thoughts, behavior, and sufferings of such doomed outcasts from colonial society. Satchell invented many characters like Bart, notably Bagstock and Drinkwood in the short stories, Andersen in *The Toll of the Bush,* and Purcell in *The Greenstone Door.* They suffer defeat and die—they are life's victims. But there is nothing evil in them, and they usually win the reader's sympathy because of some act of nobility and high moral purpose, performed at the risk or at the point of death. They are to be distinguished from his unsympathetic portraits of immoral or depraved characters, which occur especially in his first novel in Robert Brice, Cuthbert Upmore, and the unscrupulous businessman, Arthur Roller.

Hugh Clifford is Satchell's first full-scale study of the New Zealander—a new breed of man, an idealization of the rugged, outdoors man of the new South Pacific world whose manners and morals he was trying to paint. Clifford stands for the shining, optimistic side of pioneer life. He is the romantic hero of *The Land of the Lost,* drawn in a romanticism of a robuster kind than that of Geoffrey Hernshaw, the sensitive immigrant hero of *The Toll of the Bush.*

1 *Diggers and Townsfolk*

The basic source of conflict and drama in Satchell's novels is the struggle, sometimes artfully concealed, between the members of civilized society and the inhabitants of the wilderness or the bush. In *The Land of the Lost* the alliance of Robert Brice, a rough larrikin, with Cuthbert Upmore, an unscrupulous pub-keeper, to prevent Hugh Clifford from gaining his inheritance, is strengthened by the addition of Arthur Roller, a storekeeper from the township, who is Clifford's rival in love.

The gumfield itself is not evil. Though dreary and colorless, it still has a romantic aspect. It is the home of men of spiritual beauty, like Jessamine Olive, called the King of the Diggers, as well as of fellows like the good-natured aristocrat John Dopping and the attractive if tormented Bart. The gumfield is likewise the place where the hero and heroine, Hugh Clifford and Esther Hamilton, meet and fall in love. Their love is not a tragic love —despite various misfortunes it ends happily—and the key to its mood is the austere beauty of its gumfield and bushland setting. As with Egdon Heath in Thomas Hardy's *The Return of the Native*, it is the "presence" of this setting which forms a strong organic part of the novel; it is the skeleton on which the human drama is fleshed out.

The time is midsummer, about 1886. In every direction the field stretches itself out to the far horizon, covered with low brushwood, with an undergrowth of coarse, stunted fern and patches of green and orange-colored moss. It is the site of a prehistoric kauri forest, which centuries ago had taken all the goodness out of the soil before it was destroyed in some natural holocaust, leaving only the globules of gum under the ground. Now it is a barren desert of chalk-like soil, a wasteland withered by the fierce beams of the sun, where the diggers live in tents and palm shanties.

The diggers are solitary wanderers in this wasteland. Once or twice a figure bearing an empty or almost empty sack on its back, a spade across its shoulder, and a thin spear "shining like a splinter of glass" in its hand, moves across the open ground. With such spears the diggers prod the ground as they walk, searching for the lumps of gum. They are solitary figures, but many have heroic qualities.

Hugh Clifford, reflecting on the inhabitants of this antipodean Hades, thinks that the bonds of sin and failure that hold them together must be "wonderful and mysterious." He sees them as the scum and scourings of humanity, the top and bottom of the world's social system, driven to a common life in the wilderness. Many are victims of the international depression—men from English universities, settlers with hungry wives and children, unemployed mechanics and clerks, Dalmatians and Maoris, and old men for whom the world has no further use.

The three characters of major interest are Clifford himself, Bart, and Olive. Bart's attitude towards gumfield life is bitter. He sees the field as the stranding-ground of the world's deadbeats, the place where all the wrecks of the earth are thrown up to rot—"and you talk about respectability." Bart's struggle with alcohol, his effort to save Clifford, his lonely existence, make a moving narrative, while his death scene dominates the end of the book. By contrast the portrait of Clifford as a strong, clean young man, blameless and heroic, lacks depth. The ambiguity of his position on the gumfield is insufficiently realized, and it is unlikely that he would feel that "the windy world with its social exactions blew remorselessly in his face." When Bart is present the charm of his personality and the keenness of his moral judgments come through, as in the scene where he reveals to Clifford the secrets of the booze trade—Rum Number One is "given to white men," Number Two to "low whites and diggers" and Number Three to the Maoris, who "die suddenly or kill one another" since it is a mixture of "logwood, fusil oil, painkiller, and treacle."

Where Bart came from and what his past contains are not revealed, but the tragedy of his position is expressed in his cry: "In the Land of the Lost a man has no relatives, and that is the only advantage it possesses ... No death-bed relentings for me. I die game ... Give me a drink and let me die as I have lived." This is reminiscent of Captain Starlight, the Australian bushranger in "Rolf Boldrewood's" *Robbery Under Arms.*

Jessamine Olive, a man of about forty, turning grey, with a pair of twinkling blue eyes, is the antithesis of Bart, but he has a tragic wound which links him to Bart: his strange fear of the dark is a result of the deaths of his wife and child, who were killed by a falling tree before his eyes. The friendship between Olive and Bart is a kind of father-son relationship, despite their similar ages. Olive is a visionary with prophetic insight, the "only perfect Christian" on the gumfield, who believes that the world is not an easy place to live in if we do not help one another. He hears mysterious voices, sees the vanished trees all about him, and believes that angels still dwell here and there on earth.

Olive stands in contrast, spiritually, to the lightly sketched, genial autocrat, Dr. Hamilton, Esther's father, whose anger at her "adventure" with Clifford causes the scornful remark: "A gum-digger! You should have more sense." In his intolerance and lack of true feeling the old man represents the narrow values of township society, as does the fat, arrogant storekeeper, Arthur Roller, to whom Esther has already been betrothed in casual pioneer fashion.

Esther is a woman of considerable sensibility and intellectuality. Being "a motherless girl in a God-forsaken land" she had lacked guidance in making her engagement to Roller. Yet she is no foolish child; "when she meets Clifford, after her horse throws her off near his tent on the gumfield, she brings delicacy and tenderness to the story. She is not prudish either: her fear of a scandal over her visit to his tent at night is natural—"she knew the scandal-hunger of the district . . . she did not distrust him. It was the world she doubted and feared". Her sense of injustice, deriving from the upbraiding and icy politeness of her father and her fiancé, enables her to behave with strength and daring later on.

Her first decision to keep her promise to marry Roller, after she knows she loves Clifford, displays her conventional sense of honor and filial duty. But luckily Clifford's influence—that of the unconventional and vital force of the gumfield—prevails over her indecision. "You cannot give yourself where you do not love," he says. Later when Roller falsely accuses Clifford of stealing Esther's brooch, she is able to repudiate her engagement. She then defies her father and breaks free from the conventions of her upbringing—but she is helped by her discovery that her apparently worthless digger is a man of wealth and position in another part of the country.

The linking force between Esther's township standards of conduct and Clifford's gumfield romanticism is the personality of her cousin, Wilfred Hamilton. It is he who makes their love possible, and he also knows about Clifford's true social position in the distant sheepfarming district of Hawkes Bay. Hamilton is a recently-graduated doctor who took his medical degree in England and is now paying a visit to Esther. He is an "autocratic young democrat," good tempered, witty, brilliant—in fact with the makings of a prig and a little too good to be true. But he keeps Esther and Clifford together, saves Clifford's life when he is wounded, and makes sure that the wicked are punished, when the mysteries of the novel's plot are revealed. So he too contributes to the new type of fictional hero—the New Zealander —which Satchell was trying to create.

2 Opposing Worlds

The real battle of the novel's opposing worlds, with their different sets of values, takes place inside Esther's mind. Her views of the pioneer situation in Hokianga County coincide most nearly with Satchell's own. Thus her horseback ride with Wilfred Hamilton into the kauri bush, with their discovery of the Maori bush gang at work and their visit to the Maori settlement, are among the finest reflective and descriptive passages in the book, but the description is functional. Not only does Esther ally herself emotionally with the romantic world of the gumdiggers because of her "adventure" with Clifford. She also is drawn by natural sympathy to the Maori bushfallers, who are being so unscrupulously treated by their contractor, the storekeeper Roller, her unloved fiancé.

Just as the gumfield and bush inhabitants stand opposed to normal social behavior, represented by the doctor and Roller in the township, so do the gumfield and the bush represent values of the spirit higher than those in society. Because the great kauri forest and its Maori inhabitants are being exploited by Roller, and the trees that Esther loves are being cut down at his command, the proposed marriage between them is seen to be temperamentally impossible long before her personal act prevents it from taking place.

Esther expresses Satchell's deepest feelings of affinity with the vast areas of unbroken bush country where no settlers live. She worships especially the kauris—occasional symmetrical pillars which tower in stately grandeur high above the rest of the forest. She sees them as majestic beings almost with a life of their own, with a spirit or a soul, anticipating the dark pantheism of Eve Milward in *The Toll of the Bush.* In Esther's view there is something druidical about the kauris: they have as it were built themselves mounds to grow from, and such is the spread of their roots that no other trees grow near them, creating what appear to her to be "sacred" circles of bare ground. Esther tells Wilfred Hamilton that riding among the kauris is like riding through a cathedral. She loves the kauris because they are so strong and enduring and silent. Whereupon Wilfred quips that he would expect a woman to admire them on such grounds.

So it is with the Maori tree-fallers. The tree-falling scene is one that Satchell paints with the meticulous detail and vividness of a painting by the early artist Charles Heaphy. It is a rural scene, showing a primitive, peasant community at work—clearly Satchell's ideal type of community in contrast to town life. Esther is entranced by the Maoris, some of whom are falling the kauris, others cross-cutting and squaring with the broad axe logs already sawn, others yoking up a team of bullocks, and others again rolling the huge logs into position for hauling. Some lie or sit about in small groups, lazily watching the work.

This idyllic picture is reinforced by the courteous speech and behavior of the Maoris, which she contrasts with the storekeeper's avarice. It is also significant that when she rides over with the old chief Rewi to the Maori settlement, she finds that the chief's European-style house is empty. Old Rewi prefers to live in his palm-thatched, earth-floored hut. Esther too decides to sit on the ground with him.

The depraved Scarlet Man group—Upmore, Brice, and Mrs. Brandon—are really agents of the town. Upmore is Roller's representative in his dealings with the Maoris, and the hotel stands just outside the edge of the gumfield, linked to the town by the Great North Road. Clifford, Bart, Jessamine Olive, and the Maoris are not only more humane than the township group, they are also morally superior to them. Esther's alliance is a moral act, with a spiritual quality about it. The forest is like a cathedral; the Maoris are superior in terms of "human merit" to the white storekeeper with his "cashbook" standards. Even the gumdigger whom her father despises turns out to be a quixotic idealist who has refused a rich inheritance from England because the conditions attached to it offend his mother.

An attack on Jessamine Olive's cabin by Roller and Brice, and their burning down of Clifford's tent, confirm their immorality as despoilers of nature; they are condemned not only for shooting at Clifford but also for destroying the forest. The fire, steadily advancing across the inflammable scrublands, soon reaches the standing bush, and the fate of twenty miles of magnificent forest is sealed. Roller's mean spirit is shown in various other ways—by his refusal to go to Esther's assistance when she is thrown from her horse, and by his contempt for the diggers whose gum he buys and the Maori gangs of bushmen working for him.

There is a lot of rubbish talked about the Maoris' supposed nobility, according to Roller's aggressive opinion. He regards the local Maoris as a lazy, dirty lot, and has never been able to find much good in them. But his view is colored by the fact that they have run up a lot of debts which he has recorded in his store ledger.

Wilfred Hamilton, the true New Zealander, is bound to oppose such slander of the Maoris. He tells Roller that his ledger is no criterion of the merits of the Maori race. On the contrary he is inclined to pay less and less attention to the cashbook as a measure of human merit. He tells Roller that the dirtiest and laziest of his Maori bushmen would cheerfully beggar himself in the cause of hospitality, and that the best of them have a hatred of the paltriness and meanness that is associated with so much of our civilized system of money-making.

Dr. Hamilton supports Roller with another "township" view of the Maoris; he also accepts Roller's dislike at first of the gumdigger, Hugh Clifford. He speaks didactically about the Maoris, saying that there are two sides to the racial question. Admitting that the Maoris are the most intelligent aboriginal race on earth, he thinks that their intelligence will not enable them to cope with the "progressive movement" of the British settlers: they are doomed to disappear from New Zealand. This view was commonly held among many British settlers in New Zealand just then, but there is a moral flaw in such lack of vision. However, the doctor has some good feelings. When Esther pleads with him, he agrees to let her break her marriage promise to Roller, and he finally accepts Clifford as a likely son-in-law. Roller too is given some favorable qualities. He repents of his attack on Clifford and is acknowledged to be a "good businessman," but his attitude towards his Maori bushmen remains unchanged.

On the whole, then, Satchell does not absolutely reject the township people for their lack of humanity. He condemns Roller's evil use of unscrupulous men like Upmore and Brice, in his attempt to discredit and kill Clifford. Roller of course has a sexual motive here—he is inflamed by a lover's jealousy. But Roller also expresses the inhumanity of the townsmen's view of the Maoris, and is responsible for destroying the "sacred" natural beauty of the kauris. Finally, he is responsible indirectly for Bart's death, when he quarrels with him at a drunken party at the "Scarlet Man."

In his second Hokianga novel Satchell analyses more closely the contrasting claims of civilization and the wilderness, in a way that shows the conflict in his mind. But he did not return to the corrupting influence in society of mean-spirited businessmen like Roller until *The Greenstone Door,* where the theme breaks out again in his portrait of the sinister Brompart family.

So although Roller repents, and Satchell refrains from condemning him entirely, he did come to regard such behavior as Roller's in more absolute terms of opposition and hostility as his fiction developed. In his early novels he did not work out the full implication of his romantic vision of life. He was to some extent concerned, moreover, to paint a portrait of a region.

3   The Regional Flavor

The Land of the Lost has a strong regional quality in its descriptions of the Hokianga bush and tidal river country, kauri forest and gumfield, which could emerge from nowhere else in the world. There is also some use of vernacular dialect, and of the broken English speech of the Maoris, which is in various ways typical of the region. But although picturesque characters like Bart and Jessamine Olive may have been peculiar to the gumfields population of that time, the main characters and their language are stamped with a more universal pattern.

Satchell's use of language requires special comment here. One defect is a notable stiffness in the courtship scenes; yet there are also many bright, witty conversations between Esther and Wilfred Hamilton and between Clifford and Wilfred. A banal language weakness, on the other hand, is Satchell's tendency to make use of the melodramatic dialogues and confrontations of the Victorian stage. Some untypical Englishness may be noted too. "Vale" for valley; "native riders" for Maoris on horseback; "low brushwood" instead of teatree scrub; and the "inn door" (when no hotel in New Zealand was commonly called an inn). It is language in the melting pot.

The speech of the larrikin Robert Brice is not so much pure regional speech as a mixture of whaler talk and gumfields slang, with a certain number of Cockneyisms and Americanisms.

"Me and your mate," said the man, after a pause, "had a bit of a barney some days ago. I thought I'd just step round and bury the hatchet." He grinned, showing a mouthful of ragged teeth. "Yes, 'tain't the square thing to be on the cross-cut at Christmas-time; so I'm on the buryin' lay—that's my lay tonight. Here's the hatchet. . . . There was a mate o' mine once had a girl on the field—Sandy George his name were—but, lor' bless you, he couldn't keep 'er; she just passed round, you know. You'll be thinking of givin' your mate the chuck by-an'-by."

"I am Dr. Hamilton's daughter," said Esther. "What I have told you is true. I am here as the result of an accident."

"Of course," said the man, with a sneer; "accident's the word. I've been there before. Bless you, I'm not so green as I'm cabbage-looking, though dang me if ever I saw quite such a pretty style on the field. But look 'ere, missy . . . I'm not goin' to get you into no scrape with your mate, so give us a kiss and I'll sheer off right away." [1]

This conversation in Clifford's tent on the gumfield, at night by flickering firelight, shows how the vernacular phrases, "me an' your mate," "had a bit of a barney," "thought I'd just step round," "'tain't the square thing to be on the cross-cut," are enriched by the Americanism "bury the hatchet" and by the Cockney "that's my lay tonight." Similar idiomatic phrases like "accident's the word," "give us a kiss," "right away," contrast with the American "I've been there before" and the Cockney "I'm not so green as I'm cabbage-looking." However, "quite such a pretty style" and "get you into no scrape" sound less authentic from the lips of a man like Brice. "Sheer off" is seamen's speech, while "bless you" and "dang me" are obvious euphemisms.

On the whole Satchell's characterization of Brice by his speech is vivid but uncertain. The same judgment applies to Maori speech. His narrative comment has the hard clarity of a Lindauer painting, but his reproduction of Maori conversation is smudgy and doubtful, even the "r" for "l" in Rora (for Roller).

The Maoris were all in European costume, the men being clothed in the ordinary slop tweeds of the local stores, while the women and girls were robed in prints and other cheap and generally gaudy fabrics. A few of the older women had babies on their backs, closely enveloped in plaid shawls, while a number of older children ran in and out among the legs of the crowd. . . .

"Mita Rora," said the chief, addressing Wilfred in broken English, "very good man in some tings, I s'pose so; but to the Maori, no good. Ehoa (friend), sometimes ago we make contrac' with Rora; he say I buy so many tausand feet, I pay you so muttee. He say you bring so many every week; if you no bring, I make you pay all the same the fine. . . . Rora very angry man; he too hard altogether; he say, 'Pay up fine'. Then the Maoris tell, 'Too many dead body at our place that times'. Rora, he say, "Damn um dead body—where my logs?" Then the Maori very cross man too." [2]

The decline of ancient Maori culture is referred to in the bone-scraping episode, when the local Maoris bring some of their ancestors up from the Kaipara and are preparing the bones for burial. Esther explains the incident to Hugh Clifford, telling him that the bone-scraping ceremony used to be, and still is to some extent, a religious ceremony among the Maoris. It once bore some relation to the after life and to the peace of the dead person's soul. But today, she believes, the young Maoris look upon the bone-scraping and similar ancient religious practices merely as occasions for gorging themselves with meat and kumeras (sweet potatoes) at the accompanying feast. She considers their lack of appreciation is due to the influence of the ideas of the white settlers, and by implication to the Christian teaching of the missionaries who disapproved of the old Maori religious rituals.

The juxtaposition of the bone-scraping episode with the gum-scraping of the diggers at the end of the book is more than an example of the regionalism of *The Land of the Lost*. It is also one of Satchell's pieces of unobtrusive underlining. There are other discreet touches of this nature, such as the mysterious presence of the brown owl (called the morepork by the settlers) at certain points of the narrative. But on the whole the novel is not particularly rich in imagery.

There is much comedy, however. Two good comic set pieces are the description of the country race meeting in Chapter XIII, and the drunken party (previously mentioned) at the "Scarlet Man" pub. A splendid minor character in the novel, with the makings of a real comic grisette, is Maria, the halfcaste Maori servant in Dr. Hamilton's household. She is only lightly sketched in, unfortunately, for the novel would have been richer for any increase of her appearances in its pages.

Maria is important to the novel for another reason, despite her minor role. She is a representative of another new type of New Zealander, the first product of a fruitful union between the townspeople and the bush dwellers. She is a big handsome woman, and she is also amorous—a desperate flirt, in fact. But her shrewd commonsense, and her broad, tolerant humanity as well as her strong moral sense, mark her as a notable result of the inevitable intermarriage between white settlers and Maoris. In Maria Satchell sees a good omen for the future of New Zealand.

Satchell's generally optimistic view of things in *The Land of the Lost,* despite the poignancy of Bart's death, is expressed by Jessamine Olive at the end. Jess can see a better day coming as the settlers extend their landmarks and take root in the new land, like the trees they are displacing. As the gumfield is worked out the settlers move on to new parts of the wilderness. Jess sees the apple orchards and vineyards of the future, in a time when the reckless, hopeless, and unhappy inhabitants of the gumfield are all gone, when there will be only the sound of settlers' wives singing and their children playing in a happy, rural pioneer community closely linked with nature, and with over everything the peace of God. This vision of the future in Hokianga can be accepted as Satchell's vision. In *The Toll of the Bush* he gives a vivid painting of such a community, and a more searching analysis of its manners, morals, and general conditions of life.

4 Settlers on the River

Satchell's method in both his Hokianga novels is to bring into the pioneer community a man from the outside world, well-educated or of good social standing, who loses his status in the eyes of petty, conventional frontier society. He falls in love with the daughter of a leader of the community, but is temporarily frustrated because he is not valued at his true worth. This pattern, which can be seen clearly in the narrative fabric of *The Land of the Lost,* is woven even more brightly through the rather somber story of *The Toll of the Bush.* This second novel reveals how much Satchell himself must have been appalled by the provincialism of New Zealand society in the 1890s after the sophistication of his London experiences. Indeed, one of the characters in *The Toll of the Bush* points out that the whole of New Zealand has no more population than a London suburb.

If his first attempt to write a novel about Hokianga society resulted in a book of a certain thinness of texture and a comparative lack of depth, he enriched his work with a new depth of feeling and a new intellectual toughness in *The Toll of the Bush.* But his earlier optimism is darkened by a brooding sadness, hesitation, and doubt about the value of civilization, matching the mood of his youthful letters to Allan Fea.

Geoffrey Hernshaw, his new hero, is more elaborately portrayed than Hugh Clifford in *The Land of the Lost,* and more

central to the meaning of his artistic vision. Geoffrey is an Englishman with family ties on the Hokianga. His brother Robert
was born and grew up there. His dead father and mother had
earlier emigrated there, leaving him to be reared by an uncle in
London. When the novel opens Geoffrey and Robert are working a small bush farm on the river. It is a life which Geoffrey
hates, and when he thinks of the dull existence of the local
township—"a lot of young-old men, half of them bachelors, living a life of drift and satisfied"—he feels deep despair: "the lust
for something better is gnawing my heart out." He wants civilization.

A picture of the craving for knowledge, the desire for intellectual talk, for culture, which must have been a very real lack
in early New Zealand, is a major aspect of the social criticism
in *The Toll of the Bush*. The focus of it here is Geoffrey's box
of books which stands unopened in the brothers' spare room,
its lid covered with "a camp oven, a bag of staples, a couple
of rusty ploughshares and other miscellaneous ironmongery."
The day that Geoffrey takes from the box his copy of Darwin's
The Origin of Species and lends it to Eve Milward, marks the
beginning of his release from bush farming. He becomes eventually Eve's husband and co-owner with Eve's brother Sandy
of the rich 5,000-acre sheep and cattle station of their father,
Major Milward, after working for a period as his storekeeper.
From the same box Robert Hernshaw takes Green's *Short History of England* and Shakespeare's *Plays,* to help educate and
entertain his young fiancée Lena Andersen. There is something
delightful in the picture of these two reading *King Lear* in the
bush house together, and their love affair forms a lyrical part
of the novel, subsidiary to the main plot with which it is linked
by the figure of Lena's unhappy father, Sven.

Once more the conflict is between the forces of civilization
and the wilderness. The stabilizing center of the action is the
old pioneer Major Milward with his big homestead, Wairangi,
by the village of Rivermouth (Opononi). Although he is a non-
believer with "advanced views" in matters of religion, he is a
humane, generous man, more likeable than the local clergyman,
Mr. Fletcher, who is Geoffrey's rival in his love for Eve. The
Major, with his sun helmet and his cigar, his games of chess and
his account books, is a genial autocrat rather like Dr. Hamilton.

Aged about eighty but physically "as active as a boy," he was one of Hokianga's first white settlers and now "he owns half the county, and what he doesn't own he's got a mortgage on." He is the big boss.

In the loneliness and uncertainty of his exile in Hokianga, Geoffrey sees the Major's homestead, Wairangi ("the heavenly waters") as a kind of paradise:

Away in the sun-haze to the west the sand dunes of Wairangi blazed like pyramids of gold . . . His mind's eye saw the flashing casements, the deep, cool verandahs, the subtropical flower garden, the woods and orchards in which the house was embowered. Peace was there if anywhere in the world . . . Such a splendour of light lay over the scene that he might well have been gazing into Paradise itself.[3]

When this passage is related to Geoffrey's hatred of the bush, which at one point is compared to Dante's Inferno, another pattern is apparent in the novel's structure. But if Eve Milward is intended to be equated with the Biblical Eve, by an ironic reversal typical of Satchell's technique, the Serpent in this paradise is not the young agnostic with his copy of Darwin's *The Origin of Species* but the revivalist clergyman, the Reverend T. Fletcher, "a tall man of dark complexion" who claims to have converted to his fanatical brand of faith every man, woman and child among the Maoris in the Waiomo Valley.

Fletcher is not one of those clergymen defeated by rationalist scholarship, so common in Victorian literature. But he is corrupt, and his corruption lies more in the personal arrogance and unscrupulousness which lead him to lie and cheat in order to win Eve's love. He is in fact a bad priest, who is to some extent redeemed by the manner of his death. Old Major Milward shrewdly sees through him when he says: "The Church of England appointed him down here—to get rid of him, I expect." In a sermon on the beach with the Maoris gathered in a great circle around him, when he makes a subtle attack on Geoffrey in order to turn Eve away from him, he debases himself and betrays his calling by using his religion for a personal advantage. Geoffrey's only weapon is his agnosticism, but doubt is not strong enough.

If "society" in the novel is represented by the inhabitants of

Wairangi, the adjacent village of Rivermouth, and the unnamed township nearby, the opposing group are the local poor, hard-working bush settlers who correspond to the gumfield outcasts and Maoris of *The Land of the Lost*. For them the bush is "hell," for they can hardly make a living in the "black, bush-covered lands." They live in slab huts in tiny clearings "dwarfed into insignificance by the immensity of the virgin landscape from which they had been hewn." It is like "The Great Unemployed Scheme" again.

The main protagonists among the bush dwellers, apart from the Hernshaw brothers, are the Andersens and the Girds, who "occupied the outpost, so to speak, of the little army of pioneers." South of the Girds' section the wild bush country extends un-broken, roadless, and uninhabited, for forty miles. Mrs. Gird is a tall, strong woman whose crippled husband had been struck down and paralyzed ten years ago by a falling branch. She is a matriarchal figure, a woman of wisdom, compassion, and loyalty, who remains steadfast and calm and never reveals the wound to her spirit caused by her husband's helplessness. She is a sort of bush oracle who is consulted by the various characters in the story about their love problems.

Contrasted with her is Mrs. Andersen, faded and worn out, with her drunken husband Sven, and their crowd of children dressed in flour bags. Although she leaves her husband and takes her children to live with another settler named Beckwith, Satchell demands that his readers make a fresh moral judgment of her.

By all the canons of ethics as it is preached this should have been an unhappy woman; but . . . never . . . had she eclipsed the radiance that now possessed her . . . Her face, fuller and more youthful-looking than of old, was bright with health and contentment. If she ever entertained fears or regrets there was no sign of such on her countenance now.

She is true love's avatar.

Sven Andersen is a typical frontier outcast, both a foreigner and an alcoholic. "He was an alien in a strange land; an outcast, of whom none thought, for whom none cared. No place called to him. He was homeless . . . Where, then, should he go?" Although

his despair is movingly presented by Satchell, it is better to
quote from his magnificent but doomed effort to redeem himself
in the eyes of his wife and children.

For three months Andersen had been employed on the new road
which was being cut through fifty miles of dense primeval bush to
the gumfields on the Kaipara river. Winding through dark valleys . . .
the pioneers of civilisation forced their way ever farther and farther
from the settlements into the gloom of the forest. . . . As the long
cross-cut saw drove through the wood, as the American steel axe
circled and fell, he conjured up the scenes of that second wooing,
when he should break through the sullen humour that enveloped her
. . . What he yearned for was her respect, that she should point to
him with pride: 'My husband, the best bushman in the country'. And
with respect would come love . . . With the rehabilitation of the man
came a violent disgust at his past self, quivering along the haft of
the tool and biting deep with the cutting edge.[4]

Despite the inclusion of these "lost" characters in the Hokianga
novels, Satchell is on balance neither an optimist nor a pessimist,
but takes both attitudes as it suits him. Thus Wickener, the vis-
itor from England in *The Toll of the Bush* who has a vindicative
hatred of Geoffrey because of his wife Laura's alleged affair
with him years before—"a man of thirty-five with a fair skin, a
trim brown beard, and singularly bright eyes"—plays an ambiguous role. He is a wry, likable rogue and his attitude to life
is mellowed by the events of the novel. If he is sophisticated
and slyly humorous in his conversational sallies, in general his
thinking reflects the cynicism and pessimism of the Old World,
and he excuses his moral weakness by uttering such profundities
as: "God knows the human race is a set of damned fools, especially the men . . . Nothing matters . . . Rattle it as you will,
the game is in the box. That's fatalism." Or: "A good-looking
woman . . . without means of support is, owing to the inherent
vileness of human nature, subject to special temptations." But
his hate for Geoffrey is wiped out and his spirit is purified by
his friendship with the bush girl, Lena Andersen.

5 *The Cost of Civilization*

Eve Milward is the link between the novel's two contrasting
groups of people, just as she is the pawn between the religious

enthusiasm of Fletcher and the agnosticism of Geoffrey and her father. Her affection for the bush points the way to her eventual union with Geoffrey rather than Fletcher. For Eve the bush, not Wairangi, is "paradise" and it is in the bush, finally, that the two lovers come together. For Eve, as with Esther in *The Land of the Lost*, "hell" lies in the destruction of the bush, whether by axe or by fire, that is, by the advance of civilization. She finds peace and "true love" when she goes into virgin bushland.

Eve looked around her with musing eyes. The yellow road, blotted here and there with shadow, wound gradually downwards through the unbroken forest. On its margin, fern-tree and palm and springing sapling formed a continuous curtain of greenery at the feet of the lofty trees. A sweet earthy odour mingled with the honeyed breath of a myriad flowers . . . No jarring sound broke the serene peace of this temple of life.

Compare the above with Geoffrey's earlier reflection on the Wairangi homestead as a place of peace and paradise, then contrast it with the following account of the Gird's bush farm.

Eve looked around her, her face still and pale, at a loss for words. At the evidences of toil everywhere, the blackened trees, the fallen logs, some with deep axe marks in them, the wilting grass among the stumps. Then, the untouched virgin forest, the tree ferns, the rata . . . it seemed that the task set was too great, that God had forgotten.[5]

To Lena Andersen too in a minor way, after the influence on her of her drunken father and her adulterous mother; the bush is like a lost happiness. "The bush stood black and insoluble; it seemed impossible that the entrance to it could ever be found again." This first hints at the search for a door of love.

Eve not only expresses the author's romanticism, it is she too who brings up the idea that the bush has a kind of supernatural power by which it can revenge itself on mankind for destroying it, though Satchell has already expressed this in his own voice much earlier. "Every bushman knows the toll of blood demanded by the virgin forest. It is fixed and inexorable, and though skill in bushcraft will carry a man far in the avoidance of accidents, it counts for nothing when the time comes for the bush to demand its price." Later, when Geoffrey tells Eve that soon the bush country will be all cleared for settlement:

"I hope I shall not live to see it," she said passionately.
"Yes, civilisation is a ruthless thing. One is sometimes tempted to ask if it is worth the cost, but we are bound to believe so. That is a thing we dare not disbelieve."
"What wonder if it be true, as the bushmen believe, that the forest demands its toll of the destroyers. It needs no stretching of the imagination to believe that in this great silent outburst of life there is a soul that can offer resistance." [6]

This is the idea on which the novel is based. And when the great Hokianga bushfire is started later on by the drunken Andersen, the old bushman Stephen expresses the superstition again.

The old bushman seated himself and spat thoughtfully into the fire. "It's a bad business," he said, "and there's worse ahead. You bet, we're not coming through this without a price . . . I'm talking about what I know. There's a spirit in these forests same as in a man. It ain't the new chum that comes slashing at the bush without knowledge and takin' risks that would make his flesh creep if he knew of them, that pays the price. It's the man that has mastered the trade, or the man that never tried to learn it, and it's on such as them that the blow's goin' to fall now." [7]

Satchell wrote nothing better than his chapter on the Christmas festivities at the Wairangi homestead, with the big wool-shed dance and the party up at the house for the older people who yarn about the days of Heke's War. The way in which the dance draws the whole rural community suggests the real solidity of pioneer Hokianga life, with its mingling of whites and Maoris, all sheltered and bound together by the pastoral wealth of the big sheep and cattle station owned by Major Milward.

The boys on the station were getting the big shed ready for a dance, for it was Christmas Eve. The wool, gum, and lumber had been shifted out the day before, and buckets of hot lime, boiled with chopped hide, brushed on the roof and walls. The shed had a solid floor of narrow planks, well laid on heavy blocks, and was spacious enough to accommodate the largest band of dancers likely to be drawn together in the district. The whitening and scrubbing being over, a stable-lad was busy suspending large kerosene lamps from the rafters, while another young man, under the direction of Eve, was engaged in looping up garlands of waiwaikoko, or owl's-foot moss, together with branches of the Christmas tree, aflame with their blood-red flowers. An air of mirth prevailed in the building; jests and laughter passed from lip to lip, and echoed from the walls of the hollow shell . . . A large heap of greenery was piled in the centre of the room, and a number of well-dressed Maori girls were rapidly twisting it into garlands. The floor had been powdered with ground rice and was already becoming slippery from the constant trampling of the workers as they moved to and fro.[8]

Notwithstanding, the controlling pattern of the story operates here as elsewhere. When Geoffrey is spurned by Eve, he dances with one of the beautiful halfcaste Mallow girls until he is stifled by the smell of the greenery decorations, which remind him of the hellish bush life he'd hoped to escape from through his love for Eve.

There is a morbid activity of the senses attends a troubled mind. Geoffrey was unpleasantly conscious of the heavy, sickly odour of green leaves, the acrid smell that dwells in the dense bush, where the light is dim and a deathly stillness prevails.

Consequently he leaves the woolshed and goes up to the house, where Sandy Milward drinks a toast to the Maoris.

Major Milward was in his element. All the old identities of the county, rich and poor alike, were present. Withered old men with rosy cheeks, whose eyes many a time had looked squarely into the face of death— men whose memories went back to the beginning of things when the authority of the Maori chieftain was a stronger law than the Queen's. Grizzled, tongue-tied giants who knew only the cult of bush and river, but knew that with the intimacy of an instinct. Little wizened sailor men, with huge broad-chested sons already well past middle age, whalers or deserted men-o'-war's men, it may be, whose talk was of the *Eliza Jane* or the *Rose* of Bristol and of stirring adventures in low latitudes, even yet only partially explored. Frail, stooping veterans, talking familiarly of university boat-races away back in the 'forties, and cackling in high-pitched voices over jokes that had been dead and buried for a couple of generations. There was the burly form of John Manders, descended from the great missionary family, and owning twenty thousand acres of the richest land in the North country. There was Captain Russell, that prince of half-castes, dark, handsome, portly, held in honour by both races from the North Cape to the Bluff. There, again, his round old face wreathed in smiles, was little Tom Welch, the butt and boon companion of all ages, who had made and squandered at least three fortunes, and had not a vice in his composition, nor a regret.

"All the tribes," Sandy said. "God bless 'em!" [9]

Geoffrey broods on the vitality of these original pioneers, who have captured his imagination, and here Geoffrey clearly speaks for Satchell himself:

These were the heads and bodies of strong and resolute men—men who laid hold with two hands, men whose deep chests spoke of mighty organs and the power to achieve great desires by the force of great vitalities . . . Woe to the man who, in this new land, struggling with the giant forces of nature, should stand to count the cost or ask himself what he desired. Woe to him to whom a succession of obstacles brought not fresh lust of battle but the apathy of despair.

Inevitably the movement of this novel too sweeps away from organized, established society at Wairangi to the "primeval solitudes" of the bush. Thus when Eve and Mr. Fletcher go to Auckland, their stay in the little city is only an interlude, treated with irony. Also the period between Christmas and March 18th, the date of Eve's wedding to Fletcher, is occupied not with wedding preparations but with Andersen's struggle toward redemption on the new southern bush road. The great bush fire which destroys the bush coincides with the wedding which destroys Geoffrey's hope of marrying Eve himself.

Satchell's power as a writer is striking in the narrative of the bushfire, which is presented in images of vividness and horror, and in his equally clear and polished description of the wedding guests, both white settlers and Maoris. Among the Maoris he points out the difference between the old and young generations—the younger people are "Hail fellow well met" with everyone while the elders are stately and well-mannered. "Their manner toward the Europeans was marked by a charming courtesy and dignity, that aboriginal mingling of self and sympathy on which all manners, whether of courts or backwoods, are founded." Here again is evident Satchell's obsessive belief in the noble savage and natural man, which had such a profound effect on his conception of his last novel, *The Greenstone Door*.

Satchell's deepest perceptions of the nature of pioneer life are expressed in his account of the bushfire and of the subsequent struggles of the lovers, Geoffrey and Eve, through the Hokianga kauri bush for several days after Eve has run away from her husband in desperation following the wedding ceremony. Here for instance is Geoffrey's reaction to the gorge filled with supplejack vines in which he and Eve are trapped after skirting the fire and roaming through rugged, virgin bush country.

Casting its black canes from tree to tree, scrambling across the ground, turning and twisting snake-like on itself, this hellish vine added the final touch of horror to the scene. The dead, sooty blackness that had displaced the vivid green of fern tree and palm, the distorted and suffocating saplings seeking to break upwards from that pit of terrors, the hideous fungoid growths like huge cancers on the trees, the chill air, the ominous rattling of the canes—formed together a scene in which the imagination of a Dante would have revelled.[10]

But from the pit of hell the lovers achieve their paradise together. The sustained strength of the writing in the long sequence where the lovers are lost in the bush leads naturally to the climax where they fall asleep together in a fern hut, while outside by their blazing campfire "The deep monotoned ko-ko of the abounding morepork came with a profound significance, breaking the silence as [if] it were the opening of a tragic door."

What is the meaning of the phrase "a tragic door"? The tragedy does not lie in the adulterous sin, as Geoffrey now makes love to Eve. Satchell has here finally resolved his novel's conflict of antithetical forces. In metaphor, Geoffrey's conquest of Eve in the fern hut reflects the dominance of Wairangi or "society" values over the natural values of the bush which Eve loves, and which Satchell also prefers. The little campfire can be seen as a microcosm of the great bushfire, that disastrous product of civilization's inexorable march "in endless procession over trunk and bough" into the wilderness. The morepork's cry sounds like the opening of a door to tragedy because "civilization is a ruthless thing," because there is tragedy in the destruction of the bush, in a loss of innocence and beauty, and in the toll of valuable lives from among the pioneers. But once the bush is gone, farmlands can be created, to bring to New Zealand the needed pastoral wealth of sheep and cattle stations like Wairangi, of which Geoffrey becomes co-owner when he marries Eve. Nevertheless, the tragedy occurs, and in a human sense it affects most deeply the Maori inhabitants of the bush, as Satchell had already pointed out in his unpublished verse play, *Hemeroma,* and was to point out again in *The Greenstone Door,* the climax of his art. But on the whole *The Toll of the Bush* represents the victory of civilization and the supremacy of science and progress.

6   *Rebels and Outcasts*

The agnostic position taken by Geoffrey is typical of many heroes of Victorian fiction. It was a mark of intellectual freedom. It may have been inevitable, then, that the argument between Geoffrey and Eve on the question of science versus religion should end in stalemate. This debate is the least original part of the novel, but it has a philosophical tone, a quality of intellectuality, related to the book's basic ideas. Thus Geoffrey compares science to "the making of a road into the unknown," and tells Eve that science is "the formed road men call knowledge." In a way, then, it is as logical for Fletcher, the exponent of religion carried to excess who denies the values of science, to be killed in the bushfire as it is for Andersen, the doomed outcast who fails to profit from his work on the new road, to be killed by the same fire.

The concern with Maori life in *The Toll of the Bush* is not so great as in *The Land of the Lost,* although as bush-dwellers they are again shown as being dislocated by the advancing force of civilization. One of Satchell's clearest passages of scene-painting occurs, as already mentioned, in his account of the Maoris attending Eve's wedding at Wairangi, where the difference between the old and new generations shows how the innocence, vitality, and human worth of the ancient Maori culture have been lost through a crude imitation of white man's behavior.

But in this novel there is another of Satchell's characteristic reversals. The main Maori personage, Pine, is at first, in the ploughing and bootmaking episodes, presented as a comic figure.

Yet at the end it is Pine who heroically leads the search for
the lost lovers, and who finally becomes a wealthy member of
society with his own house and farm. He even manages to assert
himself against the Englishman, Wickener.

"Show them the stuff you are made of, Pine," said Mr. Wickener,
laying his hand on his protégé's shoulder. "We've got to reach them
tonight, and you are the boy to do it."
But Pine drew himself erect, and shaking from his person the
detaining hand of the white man, regarded him with the offended
dignity of the savage. Then he spoke in a low swift voice in his own
liquid tongue and turned away.
"What does he say?"
Sandy looked embarrassed. "He says you are to keep behind. He
has no time to talk with children." [11]

Inevitably the deep-seated allegiance of Satchell's temperament to his social outcasts, bushmen, impoverished pioneers, and
Maoris, causes him to side with them when they break ordinary
moral codes in search of happiness, because he knew how little
comfort there was in their tough world. "Wait till you have been
through what I have been through and then see how much
morality is left in you," says Mrs. Andersen. Her happiness with
Beckwith is a sign of Satchell's approval of those who rebel
against the conventions of organized society for a sufficient
cause. Thus, Mrs. Gird, who suffers her own tragic humiliation
in silence, approves of Lena Andersen's love for Robert. "I am
on the side of true love every time, and not blindly, but with all
the light God has given me. When I see it pure and unselfish,
then I know that I am in the presence of a thing that is beautiful and holy, and I would array myself on its side though all
the conventions of the world were leagued in opposition." Lena
herself is a splendid picture of a warm-hearted young pioneer
girl, who knows from her own hard childhood what life can do
to people. "We take pain to our hearts as a matter of course, but
we walk round happiness with suspicion."
The regional quality of the work stands out in the portraits
of minor characters such as Robert, Lena, Pine, or the old bushman, Stephen. In Stephen's remarks about the bush taking its
toll, the bushman's life is implicit in his phrases, his speech
rhythms, and his vernacular words and idioms, while Pine's

Maori patois is an improvement on Satchell's earlier renderings of Maori speech. There is little stiffness in the dialogue. The conversations move smoothly and even wittily. It is all better art than before.

Yet the book has a curious structural defect. Chapter XXVII, describing Eve's visit to Auckland, is misplaced chronologically. At the end of the three or four weeks that go by in this chapter the story has still not reached the point of time in the previous chapter where the bushfire destroys Beckwith's house and kills Andersen. A simple solution would be to place Chapter XXVII before Chapter XXV, but this would not cover completely Satchell's clumsy use of the time shift.

Another dubious side of the work is the characterization of the women, especially the young heroine, Eve. Eve, Esther—and Isabel and Helenora in his next two novels—are on the whole figures of romance rather than reality: headstrong, beautiful, fastidious girls of high social position and good breeding, of sweetness and charm, of timidity and fidelity. It is with his older, doomed or outcast women that Satchell succeeds in creating more realistic portraits. The reader's sympathy, as a result, must go less to Eve, because of her coldness, than to the adulterous Mrs. Andersen, the stoical Mrs. Gird, and the suffering, suicidal Lena—even to the halfcaste Mabel Mallow or Maria the servant, who have been drawn with more warmth. Eve is in fact a woman of considerable passion as well as intellectuality, yet with her blue eyes and long fair hair falling below her waist, she has the radiance of a dream girl, not quite real.

Satchell's acceptance of Mrs. Andersen's adultery reflects his largeness of view and his humane vision of life in general with its long humiliation of the spirit. His sympathy with his poor, driven, oppressed, and "lost" characters does not lead him to any specific social remedy, but indicates a need for reform in the moral nature of people in general. This was the ethical mission at the heart of his fiction. His indecision about the value of nineteenth century civilization enabled him to present that civilization as a complex entity, while the subjective quality of his novels was a part of his attempt to be true to life as he knew it from his experiences in early New Zealand, as well as being a product of the pervasive, implacable romanticism of his art.

CHAPTER 4

The Magic Serum

THERE is a strong strain of fantasy in Satchell's fiction. In his next novel, *The Elixir of Life*, his fantasy world takes precedence over the realism of his Hokianga stories and novels. The debt to Hawthorne's *Septimus Felton* is negligible, and the date of events is around 1906. Besides being the story of a scientific miracle, *The Elixir of Life* is, as already mentioned, the story of a voyage, it is based on Satchell's own voyage out. The voyage aspect of the novel is the most interesting part of a theme showing confusion of the earlier context of exile and non-return so prominent in the Hokianga novels.

More than the Hokianga novels, *The Elixir of Life* is a book with two heroes. Just as *The Land of the Lost* had its two antithetical or complementary characters, the friends Hugh Clifford and Wilfred Hamilton, so *The Toll of the Bush* had its two brothers, Geoffrey and Robert Hernshaw, as two sides of the same coin—the sturdy, unthinking, ignorant bushman and the sensitive, educated, doubting older brother who hates the bush. In *The Elixir of Life* the pattern of relationship between the two friends Alan Vincent and Philip Westland is different again, like Quixote and Sancho Panza.

In *The Elixir of Life* the voyagers are wrecked on an island. There is no direct resemblance to the North Island of New Zealand on which Satchell spent his fifty-six-year exile from England, but the connection is there. His sick hero, Philip Westland, is cured by the marvelous elixir which the island possesses, just as Satchell himself was healed, in a more subtle way, of the malaise which drove him from England, by his experience in the Hokianga bush.

Now the scientist hero, Alan Vincent—a figure vaguely idealizing Satchell's old friend Allan Fea—makes the elixir work in medical terms. The book ends with Vincent and Westland and their wives returning to England, where Vincent is honored for his contribution to science by the men of the Pasteur Institute, though privately he does not know whether his contribution is the gift of a god or a devil.

But it is this element of return to England and Europe—instead of going on to New Zealand to live as originally intended—which gives an air of falsification to the climax of the book. Insofar as it is a product of Satchell's own experience, the story has a quality of dream or wish-fulfillment about it which the actual fantasy of the elixir cure-all reinforces. Thus *The Elixir of Life* represents the reverse or regressive side of Satchell's art as a novelist; it breaks with his genuine achievement as a painter of the new world of transplanted British manners in the Pacific region. As such it is a secondary work in his canon.

Nevertheless, it contains much excellent writing. It shows again ability for characterization in depth, in the two leading male characters and their lively, loving, sweet-tempered women. An assured narrative prose is matched by some passages of witty dialogue. But there are also a number of places where there is a fall in the quality of the writing—a kind of lack of maturity, or weariness—a tendency to dubious philosophizing and over-romantic descriptions. All this suggests that the book was rewritten from notes and reflections made on Satchell's actual voyage of 1886.

The novel is divided into two sections. Part I, "On the Vessel," establishes the personal relations of the various young people on shipboard. Part II, "On the Island," deals with the fantastic events which occur after the ship is wrecked on the uninhabited islet in the South Indian Ocean. The medical discoveries and researches on the island, though presented in a realistic enough fashion, arouse the reader's resistance for the simple reason that the concept of the elixir cannot appeal seriously today to an adult mind.

The simplified ending, in which Alan Vincent is given a hero's welcome on his return to England, somewhat negates the moral drawn in the story about the vanity of scientific knowledge and the tendency of absolute power to corrupt even the most idealistic of men. Perhaps the best aspect of this novel is its incidentally satirical intention—the idea of an anti-Utopia in the community set up by the castaways on the island. There the politician on board, the Honorable Smithson, Minister of Immigration for New Zealand, becomes a humble rations clerk, while the ignorant clerk, Street, becomes the island's dictator.

Street is a character capable of greater development. He is an opportunist, a type of the new revolutionary, a Bazarov who cannot feel. One sees that Satchell could have made much more of him, to the novel's advantage. He foreshadows in some ways an Orwellian state organizer or Big Brother type. His coolness in action and his ruthless handling of the castaways have as well sinister implications which are not brought to any satisfactory conclusion. He remains the man of tomorrow, the new man of the new world who grows in stature as soon as he emigrates from England's restrictive social pattern. Yet there is also something about him of the submerged Stalinist.

Men did not openly mention his name, using rather some such phrase as "They're going to" or "They want us to lend a hand at", and Street preferred that it should be so. It seemed to be only in an idle and jocular mood that he suggested chalking a notice on the ship's side to the effect that any person found on board would be shot, yet it was done, and from the day of its appearance, unsigned and authoritative as it appeared, it was obeyed to the letter.[1]

His domination of the castaways is also explained by his inexhaustible energy and his unshakable assurance of success, and his perennial flow of ideas. He is in fact a natural dictator who needed only the right circumstances to bring out his menacing talent.

1. *Romantic Hero*

On the morning of the 3rd of August, toward the end of the Northern Hemisphere summer, the steamship *Waima* of 6,500 tons leaves the Bay of Biscay behind on her voyage to New Zealand. The *Waima* is travelling via Capetown and Hobart, and it is to be the most eventful voyage of the little ship's career, down through the Atlantic and across the South Indian Ocean. Some of the passengers are bound for Tasmania, but most are English emigrants and New Zealanders returning home after a trip to the "old country," England.

The most important person on board, at least in his own

estimation, is the Honorable William Smithson, New Zealand's Minister of Immigration, returning after a successful mission to obtain workers to help build New Zealand's new central railway system, the Main Trunk Line. The despised clerk, Street, is seeking a new life in New Zealand as a farmer, or as it is put in the story, a "rousing, chest-opening life among equals." The reversal of roles of these two after the shipwreck soon gives a meaning to this egalitarian ideal.

Also on board is the Jamesian figure of Miss Pencarrow, a lady journalist who has been sent out by the London *Daily Teller*, to discover how far the conditions of the country are "the result of experimental legislation, more especially labour legislation," for this was the era of Seddon and Reeves when many advanced ideas of government were being introduced in the little colony.

Others are Mrs Fotherington, a widow who tries to flirt with the ship's captain; "Joolium," a precocious three-year-old orphan in the captain's care, who is going to stay with relatives in New Zealand, and eighty British navvies for work on the Main Trunk Line. But most important are the group of six young people— Dr Alan Vincent, a "man of genius" and "one of the marked men of the medical world at the present time"; Philip Westland, an Englishman; Isabel Vine, Grace Severne and the two Severne brothers, Henry and Harold, who are likewise all English.

In Alan Vincent, the scientist hero, Satchell returns to his conception of the ideal New Zealander as he had portrayed him in Wilfred Hamilton, and to a lesser extent in Hugh Clifford. Vincent has been to England to complete his medical researches, for to many New Zealanders at this time England was still "home," and New Zealand still "the colony." As one of the passengers says of Vincent:

"New Zealand has sent home a good many brilliant youngsters besides the 'All Blacks', but she never sent a brighter than that one. Every scholarship he went in for he won; every exam his name was at the top of the list with honours; and when he wasn't winning scholarships and such like, he was annexing athletic cups, or scoring tries, or doing the hat trick."

Vincent has already become known among scientists for "a new method of combating consumption," but like other Satchell heroes he has a secret trouble in his past, for despite his power-

ful physique, noble brows and strong, regular features, in his
eyes is a look of weariness and despair, which "belied the splendid promise of his young manhood." In other words he is a
stock romantic hero.

Philip Westland is also a romantic young hero with a guilty
or sorrowful past. Isabel Vine says to him: "I knew that you
had some great sorrow—something unforgettable, overwhelming;
something that—how shall I express it?—made all existence like
a dream to you." A good deal of mystery surrounds his actual
medical condition. This is important since he is the subject of
the experiment carried out on the island by Alan Vincent, who
makes a serum which not only cures him but gives him complete
and permanent immunity to all diseases and makes him, theo-
retically, immortal. Westland, Isabel Vine, and the three Severnes
all suffer in varying degrees from tuberculosis. Harold Severne
is the sickest, so frail that his legs appear to "float beneath him"
when he comes out on deck for a walk assisted by his brother
and sister.

The medical theme is most firmly established by Westland,
who is a neurotic with a "dual nature," for from the "deepest
bottom of pessimism the man's spirit seemed to leap suddenly
to the supreme heights of optimism." Physically he is short, slight
and emaciated. He is, in fact, a foil to Alan Vincent, and his
function in the book is to bring out for the reader's observation
the ideas and skills which Vincent possesses. Accordingly, in a
discussion of Harold Severne's condition he asks Vincent:

"What are the medical men doing? Year after year, every year with
its cry of 'eureka' and at the end—nothing. . . . How long is it since
Koch isolated the bacillus of consumption—ten years, or is it twenty?
—and you have not yet discovered how to kill it. Now to the lay
mind that seems absurd".[2]

Vincent replies that before long, diseases of the vital organs will
not be permitted to occur: "I believe that eventually men will
die only from accidents and preventable causes; there will be
no incurable diseases and no old age." Satchell then puts into
Vincent's mouth some of the curious theories about the relationship between sex and death which were current among semi-
scientific thinkers of that day.

"Man has come to regard death as a certainty, whether or no, and experience seems to bear him out; but down in the simplest forms of life there is no real death, only division. Individual death seems, in fact, to have come into the world with sex. Love and Death, the most desired and the most abhorred, seem to have entered hand-in-hand."

This does not sound like a great scientist at work, and it is clearly the voice of Satchell rather than of Alan Vincent. The tentative nature of Satchell's thinking is revealed by the frequent use of the word "seems" in these passages, which creates the impression that in moving into the field of scientific matters he was getting a little out of his depth. The result is that Vincent is less a living character than the men of the Hokianga novels, and takes on some of the qualities of a puppet designed principally to mouth the author's speculations on science and mortality.

The medical vision of immortality has an element of quackery in it, even in Alan Vincent's noble words. "But if the blood were a perfect vitaliser, completely resistant to all that is harmful, wholly beneficent in construction—and it is both of these imperfectly;—then, then—or if it could be made so—then, short of catastrophe, individual life could go on for ever." Naturally this raises the question of over-population in the mind of Westland, who objects that such an achievement could be disastrous. "Imagine the whole population of Europe, the vast hordes of Asia, suddenly becoming immortal," he says. "Or imagine such a secret in the hands of an irresponsible, monied few." Vincent reminds him of the world's falling birthrate and adds that though human beings are imperfect as yet, when a perfect type is accomplished, which is "what evolution means," then all will be well. "Pain, disease, death—the whips that scourge us to the right path—will be laid aside, and man will be as a god." The reference to men as gods and to the "whips that scourge us to the right path" reveals a streak of paranoia in Vincent's personality, which his subsequent behavior confirms. Here he approaches the "ruthless scientist" type of fictional character, much as at other times he is a Don Quixote restrained by the Sancho Panza figure of Philip Westland.

If the book's ostensible hero is Vincent, the real hero is Westland, and his shipboard love affair with Isabel Vine provides the main romantic interest. The constant idealizing tendency of the novel is most strongly marked in Westland. He is presented in some ways as a kind of Christ-like character, somewhat resembling Dostoevsky's Prince Myshkin. He radiates goodness and compassion throughout the story, and his offer to test the serum and put his life in jeopardy for the future welfare of mankind is consistent with his general behavior. He is more human, and more interesting, than his associate. His compassion shines out in his attempt to help the two sick Severne brothers, Harold and Henry. When Harold dies of tuberculosis, it is Westland who tries to comfort Henry. But Henry replies: "My brother has been dying for two years, seven hundred days, each day struggling for life. I am told that I shall take longer, but there lies my road; and it is for me to say whether I shall tread it." Westland tells Henry about the new medical "process" that Alan Vincent is working on, but his encouragement fails to save the despondent Henry, who commits suicide by jumping overboard in the night.

It is the women who see Philip Westland's true nature. Grace Severne feels that she is falling in love with him, and says to Alan Vincent: "What is the magnetism he possesses? All the men single him out; all the women are in love with him. His eyes seem to draw me into the partnership of an infinite sorrow, yet half the time he speaks in jest. Is it just goodness?" She tells Alan also that he resembles Philip in many ways, only "When you cease to be loved you will be hated, while he . . . probably will be despised." Whereupon Alan smiles and says: "That was the fate of the Christ."

Among the women Isabel Vine is the best drawn. She is another of Satchell's excellent studies of idealized women, of a similar mould to Esther Hamilton and Eve Milward: the same type of innocent, clear-eyed, keen-witted young ladies—ethereal and slightly unreal—who are so delightful even if they are the most romantic creations in his books. Eventually it is Isabel instead of Grace Severne who becomes Philip's lover. She is only eighteen, and believes that she will not live long because of the tuberculosis she suffers from.

Tuberculosis is the disease which provokes all the talk about love and death in *The Elixir of Life* and provides the focal point of the action. The ship and the island are twin or opposed

settings, with no apparent allegorical meaning, yet to some extent
the serum can be seen to be allegorical. The following remarks
by Philip Westland support this view:

"Yes, I know. Heredity is the bogey-man of the modern world, and
is fast becoming its policeman. Yet probably if a ship-load of your
incurable tendencies, male and female, were landed on some isolated
spot, where the conditions were favourable, a few generations would
yield a robust race. Nature breeds out as well as in." [3]

Here again Satchell's compelling romanticism takes over the
meaning. Nature is the best healer, so in a way the serum is an
allegory for nature. The island where the voyagers are wrecked
acquires some of the qualities of a sanatorium. But the philosophy of the book falls below the standard reached by later
novels on the sanatorium theme, such as Thomas Mann's *The
Magic Mountain*. The idea of magic is nevertheless persistent;
the serum is seen as a miracle. Alan Vincent is merely the pawn
of nature, who makes the god-given (or devil-given) magic work
for human beings.

On the ship Vincent already knows how to cure Isabel Vine.
The serum he uses is the one he had been working on in London,
but he doubts its real power. Isabel herself thinks it is Philip's
love for her that has cured her, plus the relaxation and fresh
air of the sea voyage. Much of the talk about love between these
two is of the very essence of romanticism, with all its defects
of excessive feeling. When Philip says he cannot marry her
because he is tubercular ("Isabel, as I look into the future, I see
the pale ghosts of the broken men and women who will one day
curse me for the gift of life") she says that love is what will
cure him. "The instinct of her nature told her that love was a
sacred thing. The Creator himself had lit this golden flame in
her heart; the winds of reason might blow upon it in vain." He
refuses to think of marriage. Undaunted, she links love with the
idea of God: "If the star of our love is not a light to follow,
then God has mocked us." But he replies bitterly: "Where is
God in my life?" He then meditates on his condition, in a passage which shows him to be less of a medical case than a type
of the modern sick hero, whose neurosis is a kind of *angst*. He
becomes Sartrian man.

What was it, then, that ailed him? What was this mysterious malady
that left him clear-witted, not without muscular strength, capable of
endurance, yet averse to effort, oppressed, miserable? It was as
though the chord of life had slipped into a minor key—as though in
the midst of life's vivid dream he had come upon that moment that
precedes awakening, when doubt creeps in and the splendid vision
flows into vagueness. But if life held, indeed, no worse, had he not,
after all, something to give? [4]

Writing in such a pessimistic vein was unusual even for Satchell,
but common in New Zealand fiction of his time.

Westland is one of those who can see the beauty of life, and
he is inclined to be scornful of Alan Vincent's scientific outlook
on everything. He says to Isabel when she frets over Harold's
death: "Pain and sorrow are but the setting of the jewel, the
shadow that gives consciousness of light. All things are known
by their antithesis." He is the romantic hero inspired by nature's
wonders. "As he gazed at the night sky, pain fled, sorrow vanished, the spirit of the man rose up." Spiritual rather than cor-
poreal, he regards his sick body as a burden he would gladly
get rid of. He is Christ in the Garden, Prince Myshkin in Russia.
But his liberation takes an earthly form, after the ship is wrecked
on the island. There the elixir takes control; there too the dictator Street holds sway over men's lives. And there too love,
previously unrequited, can be consummated. The island forms
a curious setting for a reconciliation of the opposing forces of
science and nature. It is the garden of innocence, the romantic
garden, where simultaneously love blooms and a scientific miracle
occurs.

2. Sex and Death

In the South Indian Ocean a storm hits the *Waima*, the pro-
peller shaft breaks, and the ship drifts for three months, like a
sort of Flying Dutchman. Once the passengers see "the green
and violet spendour" of the Antarctic ice to their south. At this
point Satchell's belief that under special circumstances men and
women are justified in breaking the social conventions is carried
a stage further. True love takes over.

During the period of drift the secret of Alan Vincent's un-
happiness is revealed: he is married to a mysterious woman on

board, known as "Mrs. Amherst," who keeps to her cabin. But they have been separated for some time. Once again nature is the touchstone of moral behavior. "On the day of our marriage disillusionment began; in a year no power could have drawn us back to one another . . . the moment love ceases marriage descends into the pit. No ceremony of religion can consecrate what nature abhors." Vincent wants Grace Severne to become his mistress. "How strong are the bonds of convention. . . . If we were great enough, if ours were the untameable souls of heroic lovers, we should rise above them into the realm of sunlight and freedom."

Sunlight and freedom are the conditions of life on the island where the ship is wrecked on December 8th, at the beginning of the southern summer. It has a low sandstone cliff, stunted trees, a reef. The ship plunges through an opening but is held up on the rocks of the inner reef. The captain is injured, whereupon Street immediately takes charge.

The more artificial the conditions, the more superficial the talents necessary to shine in them. It is amidst primitive surroundings that the deep, strong nature finds its chance, and Street, the disregarded hack of a London merchant's office, passed as naturally to command in the new conditions as he had sunk to servitude in the old.

The Honourable William Smithson, in accordance with this natural law, becomes a nonentity on the island among the three hundred shipwrecked passengers. Tents are set up and a primitive community is formed, while the ship is being repaired. Street lays down laws of behavior: no man is entitled to the use of a shelter unless his own hands have helped to build it. He introduces martial law, and hangs a passenger named Smith who had raped one of the women from the ship. A council of advisers is set up to help rule the island.

But all this, the social theme, is subsidiary to the medical events which dominate the lives of the young scientist and his friends. They first notice that the island is covered with flowers. "Every inch of the ground was carpeted with flowers. White, blue of all shades, pink, buttercup yellow, glowing purple— they spread away in a vast sheet, until the separate hues were blended and lost in one delicate mist of colour." The island is

five or six miles across, has fresh water, birds, and lizards that
live in holes in the sand, and "a small russet-coloured animal,
somewhat larger than a rabbit, that ran after the fashion of a
kangaroo." These animals carry the elixir of life in their bloodstream.

One advantage of the dictatorial rule established by Street is
that it leaves Alan Vincent "undisturbed freedom" to carry out
his researches. He uses as guinea pigs the small, kangaroo-like
animals which Westland calls a "sort of opossum." Vincent mentions to him one peculiarity of these opossums: they are un-
mistakable marsupials, but the pouch has become abortive. Like
the human tail, it is traceable but functionless, so that there are
"no perfect females" among them, nor are there any males. "Do
you mean those little chaps are actually neuters?" Westland asks.
After a while Vincent replies:

"Either I am insane or I am on the road to an amazing and incredible
discovery—one so tremendous and far-reaching that if it be as I am
almost venturing to believe, it will shake human society to its foundations, and alter the destiny of the world." [5]

He explains that he has been amazed to discover, when he injected one of the animals with the "cyto-toxin" which he had
used to cure Isabel Vine, that it had no effect as a serum. Later
injections of tuberculosis culture had no effect on the animals.
Nor did injections of such virulent diseases as chicken pox and
influenza, apart from a slight rise in the animals' temperature.
"These animals were immune from every disease with which I
could attack them; they therefore possess in their blood qualities
of resistance of a kind approaching the marvellous." From the
blood of one of them he has made his magic serum.

Vincent believes that if he injects his serum into the bloodstream of a human being it will not only cure any disease the
person happens to be suffering from, but will make him immune
thereafter to all diseases whatever. It is "something, an elixir—
a living principle, before which the armies of death must go
down like chaff before the wind." He has tested it on himself
by making colonies of various diseases, adding a drop of the
serum, and injecting the mixture into his arm with no ill effect.
Now he has decided to make his own body the battleground

by injecting the diseases into himself first and adding the serum a short time later after he has become actually ill. Westland persuades him to make the experiment on his body instead. Philip is soon mysteriously ill, and when Isabel tries to nurse him, Vincent drives her away. As he does so he thinks: "How is it that all great things require brutality for their achievement? . . . Would there be a Christ without the brutes who crucified Him?" Philip tells him to delay giving him the serum until the last possible moment. Vincent sits at his bedside recording his steadily rising temperature. "For fifty minutes the black line moved upwards, past the utmost line of danger into the regions where death has set his seal; then swerved erratically and began to fall." So Philip is cured, not only of the disease with which he had been artificially infected, but of his old tuberculosis as well. Yet he is afraid it will return: "To have hope and lose it, that would be to die twice."

Westland's Christ-like nature is emphasized when Vincent asks him if it was the thought of renewed health for himself that prompted him to risk his life in the experiment. Philip replies that it was an impulse. "I felt drawn to it. It seemed a tremendous thing for suffering humanity if it could be proved effective." He also has enough confidence in Alan to believe it will succeed.

Once again the occasional falsities of language reveal that Satchell's mind is not fully engaged, his imagination not totally committed to this vision of human destiny. When he says that the elixir is a living principle before which the "armies of death must go down like chaff before the wind" he is guilty of mechanical, tired, and unimaginative writing. These worn-out phrases have lost any real meaning and Satchell would not normally have used them. The same criticism applies to "the regions where death has set his seal." The sense of strain in these clichés suggests that Satchell himself did not really believe in his elixir; he strives too hard to be convincing and fails through his very over-emphasis. The extent of his struggle to convince himself of the impossible becomes even wider as he returns to his peculiar ideas about the relationship between sex and death.

Vincent explains to Westland that the two of them, having had the serum injected into their blood, are now immune to all further disease attacks for the rest of their lives. Furthermore, the opossums on the island, which are neither male nor female,

owe their "neuter" quality to the fact that they cannot die
naturally. They are sexless, or asexual, because their reproductive
organs have atrophied through lack of use over thousands of
years, in the same way that the kiwi cannot fly because its wings
have become vestigial through millions of years of evolutionary
living as a ground-feeding bird. Each of these opossums, moreover, on this island carpeted with flowers—which one must assume is the paradise garden of Satchell's romantic imagination
—is thousands of years old. Vincent explains once more the
scientific riddle. "Nature, lavish as she so often appears, is at
heart a niggard," he says. "She never yet gave anything for
nothing, and the moment the imperative need for any faculty or
functional organ ceases, in that moment does she begin to remove it." This is of course a well-known scientific fact.

So that is the immortality Dr. Alan Vincent has found, the
"amazing and incredible" discovery that will "shake human
society to its foundations" and "alter the destiny of the world."
In other words, Vincent and Westland, the men who have been
inoculated with the magic serum, are immortal already. Once
again the adult reader is repelled by the over-emphatic wording
of Vincent's speech, as much as by the difficulty of believing
that such a miracle could ever come to pass.

Satchell tries hard to be convincing. But his story has not
reached the full extent of its logic. He makes no comment on
his two heroes' eventual fate of sexual atrophy. It is also a situation in which Grace Severne and Isabel Vine must become
intimately involved. It is the solution which these four make of
their problems as potential immortals which forms the climax
of the novel.

3. *Among the Immortals*

The idea of immortality closely tied to religious concepts, is
as old as human life itself. In the art of fiction immortality is
a worthwhile subject, but at the same time one of the most
difficult for a novelist to deal with in a convincing manner. It
is possibly a better subject for satire than for the serious use
Satchell makes of it in *The Elixir of Life*. But he was not the
only novelist to treat it seriously, and he will not be the last.

Grace Severne is described early in the novel as having "the
face of an angel." She is thus rendered similar to Esther Hamil-

ton and Helenora Wylde, both of whom are called angels in one way or another, and to Eve Milward who is a little like the Biblical Eve. There is a touch of immortality about all these charming women—a romantic touch no doubt, but done with the lightest of brushes, so that the portraits do not suffer in this respect, at least in the other three novels. In *The Elixir of Life,* however, the notion of immortality becomes too burdensome. The Christian concept of angels as being sexless and immortal may have influenced Satchell's design. Certainly Philip Westland, with his Christ-like qualities, is a candidate for angelhood also. But Alan Vincent, with his scientific outlook, takes on more of the cynicism of a Lucifer. He does not know himself whether the elixir is the gift of a god or a devil.

The doctor notes that Philip Westland's temperature is still slightly above normal after the experiment, yet he has otherwise quite recovered. This is because his "old trouble," which he ascribes to a "sort of rebellion or inertness of the natural cells," is still being worked on by the serum so recently injected into his bloodstream. Immortality cannot be achieved in an hour or two.

The idea of the cells of the body rebelling is in line with Satchell's ideas about society being divided into those who obey the rules and conform, and those who rebel and are destroyed. The body of Philip Westland is a kind of society of natural cells. Vincent, the scientist, is the policeman who restores order in the body weakened by cellular rebellion. "Is it not possible," he asks, "that long-dormant cells have been reinspired with that spirit of order without which health is impossible; that they are building up starved nerves, toning and tuning the whole body into the major key of life?" In the end there will not be a cell in Westland's body which does not "move in complete subservience to the whole," and he will enjoy perfect health.

The small allegory here is a pleasant piece of fancy, one of the things which give Satchell's work a kind of gloss which relieves the darker textures of his prose. It also fits in with his organic theories of life as a unity. For him, wholeness is one of the most important human qualities. His characters owe their highest responsibilities to the human race as a whole.

Vincent tells Westland that he has deserved the prize of perfect health by his noble behavior: "If there be one man who has earned an immortality of well-being it is he who, in the cause of humanity, was prepared to lay down his life; the man whose heroic spirit came up from the bottomless pit to insist that the work should be well and truly done." Once again Westland is the Christ-figure who has saved mankind through his personal suffering. But once again the phrases "heroic spirit", "bottomless pit" and "well and truly done" by their very staleness raise doubts about Satchell's real belief in what he is saying. However, with Philip now free to marry Isabel Vine, (since it was only the scruple of his sickness which had kept him from marriage before), the interest of the story shifts back to Vincent's love for Grace Severne, from whom he is still separated by the existence of his estranged wife, "Mrs. Amherst."

Dr. Vincent has made himself immortal by means of his magic serum. But he now asks himself if immortality is a thing to be desired without the companionship of the girl he loves. He would have had the wonderful prospect of "an immortality of youth and love" if he had not made the mistake of a wrong marriage long ago. He rebels against the social convention of marriage and the Christian sanction reinforcing his legal bonds to "Mrs. Amherst" even when he no longer loves her. It is the battle once more against the accepted social codes, which Mrs. Andersen in *The Toll of the Bush* had violated when she decided to leave her drunken husband. Vincent wonders why "man's puny conventions" should keep him from Grace Severne. Surely she would yield to his need if he had the courage to demand what he wanted.

Her heart was on his side; only dread of the opinion of the world clogged her footsteps—the mud of the base world. His pride rose up and told him the opinion of the world could be nothing to them; the gibes of the paltry minds for whom conventions were conceived could not enter the air breathed by the woman of his choice.

The fact that the immortality of youth and love which Vincent envisages would not be love as we know it, since the physical centers of love would eventually be atrophied and love would become purely spiritual, as among the angels, can be overlooked for the more immediate concern of the effect of immortality upon Vincent's mind. The passage just quoted reveals that the young scientist has succumbed to paranoic delusions of grandeur induced by the knowledge of his scientific skills and his success as a doctor. If any confirmation is needed, it is supplied in Vincent's later reflections.

Because he believes he is now among the immortals, Vincent becomes inhuman. He is no longer a man, at least in his thinking. "He had become as a god, holding the keys of life and death. The world was there at his feet, a cringing, suppliant world, and should he hesitate to take of that world what he wanted, asking leave of no man?" This passage is so bad that one wonders about Satchell's intent in writing it. The conclusion of the book shows that he still regards Alan Vincent in a sympathetic way, but here it appears that his bias against the scientific outlook on life has roused hostility to his character.

The effect of Vincent's state of mind on his relationship with Grace Severne is predictable. He takes her on a picnic above the beach, where he tells her the story of his experiments. Tuberculosis, he says, is now "as extinct as the moa; I have wiped it out." When she says that he will be the most famous man on earth, he replies that without her as his wife all the world's honors would be worthless.

So far in the novel, Grace Severne has been a somewhat colorless person, although her physical attractiveness has been noted; she has the figure of a Venus as well as the face of an angel. But now when Vincent kisses her and says she must marry him, she refuses. She says she has always deeply loved him, since the days when he boarded at their house in London as a medical student. But she knows of his marriage to "Mrs. Amherst," and she cannot become his mistress now. "I must value my good name above all things," she says, asserting herself in a way that makes her a worthy companion to Esther Hamilton and Eve Milward in Satchell's fictional portraits of women.

Alan tries to persuade her of the futility of her attitude: they are shipwrecked people on an unknown island, and if the ship cannot be repaired they may never return to civilization. "Can a good name confer happiness?" he asks. "Poor comfort in a good name that costs you a life's love." Her reply is that of a well-bred, right-minded girl who has been taught to keep to the rules of her society, even when shipwrecked. This time she answers that, "even if I had no regard for the opinion of the world,

I must listen to the voice of my conscience. You cannot argue right into wrong." He then explains his view that "there is a hundred times more real morality in nine illicit unions out of ten than in a loveless marriage, though it be made in accordance with every law and convention." But she still insists that she hasn't the strength to throw off the beliefs in which she was brought up.

Vincent's behavior becomes progressively more repugnant. His unpleasantness as a man, despite his genius as a scientist, shows how deeply Satchell was opposed to the scientific view of the universe, and how strongly his spirit as an artist rebelled against the achievements of science. His wavering, unsure portrait of Alan Vincent is proof of his rejection of modern, scientifically-minded man. The type of man he preferred was the subject of his next novel's tragic climax—the archetypes of natural man as portrayed in the outlawed trader Purcell and the young Maori chief Rangiora.

Vincent reminds Grace Severne of all he has done for her in the past, insisting that she "must submit" to what he calls "the price of my guardianship." This moral blackmail produces the desired result: she says they must wait till they leave the island. Then "if not for love, then as a just debt," he says, "you shall be mine. On any terms you shall belong to me." He is rapidly turning into an ersatz Nietzschean superman.

Having bludgeoned Grace Severne into the promise to become his mistress, Vincent shows next an even more undesirable kind of inhumanity. His views on racial matters are totally opposed to Satchell's own thinking. "Immortality for the higher races is one thing," but for the whole host of mankind, he says, "with undiminished powers of procreation, quite another." Before the evolutionary process can take effect and the immortal humans become neuters, like the little kangaroo-like creatures on the island, the world will have become over-populated. What so-called "higher races" does Vincent refer to? Evidently Negroes and Chinese are to be excluded, as are the "riff-raff of the earth" —presumably all those who cannot meet his standards of "higher" human behavior. His hypocrisy is unacceptable, however, to Philip Westland.

The two friends clash over the problem of Vincent's estranged wife Agnes, who is still known by the other shipwrecked voyagers only as "Mrs. Amherst." When one of the men named Bornwick breaks into Vincent's laboratory, he accidentally smashes a test-tube containing the culture of a virulent disease. Agnes Vincent is able to nurse him back to health, as she is a qualified nurse. Philip Westland says Vincent must inoculate Agnes with the magic serum which will give her immortality also, "because through our act she has incurred the risk of death." Vincent at first refuses to do so, agreeing only when Westland says it will mean the end of their friendship if he does not. He persuades Vincent to give her the elixir, as he has already given it also to Grace Severne and Isabel Vine. They then argue whether to keep the whole thing a secret.

In the meantime the ship has been repaired through the efforts of Street, Captain Ross, and others. The men clear the ship of everything movable and wait for the next spring tide. Vincent reflects on his position and rebels at "the harsh fate that made of his discovery a weapon for his own undoing." Life among the five immortals is going to be an unhappy business, for how can he marry Grace Severne when Agnes will always be alive to block his desire? The only alternative is an adulterous union, but Grace rejects that also by her sudden decision to go back on her agreement with him to become his mistress after they leave the island.

The novel has now bogged down in the problems of being immortal. Immortality becomes a repugnant prospect to Grace Severne, after Alan Vincent, with unexpected high-mindedness, frees her from the bargain they had made. She reflects on her new wretchedness as she faces an endless future without the comfort of the man she loves.

Love and death alike had cast her off. A sense of infinite loneliness came over her; it was as though she had passed from the region of human affections into a land where there was no life; a place of arctic chill, of unchanging conditions, where no love was or ever could be.[6]

These sentences could form a pessimistic conclusion to what has come before them. Life without love, as neuters, is a possible ending to Satchell's fantasy of human immortality. Optimistically the novel does not end there: Grace changes her mind again, goes to Vincent and says, "Take me." Agnes Vincent tells

Alan that she will release him from their marriage by an act of adultery—the reason for her secret, incognito voyage to New Zealand is that she is going to "marry" a wealthy man living there who was a friend of her childhood; he will give her the security of a home.

Street's efforts to refloat the ship prove successful. Shortly before the voyagers leave the island, Alan Vincent and Grace Severne are "married" on board ship. Philip Westland and Vincent have also secretly inoculated Street with the elixir. As the ship sets course for Hobart, Vincent looks back at the island, which is called Llewellyn Island, and says "that some day men will regard this spot as sacred ground." He has finally decided that to withhold the elixir from any member of the human race would be the same as committing murder. Therefore he intends to make his discovery known to the world and let everyone share the doubtful joys of immortality.

The book ends with Vincent, Westland, and their wives returning to England to meet the men from the Pasteur Institute. The world has already been informed by Miss Pencarrow of the *Daily Teller* of the discovery of the elixir. Alan Vincent's last speech declares: "Heaven only knows whether what I am bringing to the world is the gift of a god or a devil." This makes it clear that he has at least partially recovered from his earlier paranoiac state.

However, the confusions in the characterization of Alan Vincent provide the clue to the book's partial failure as a work of art. Satchell muddles the ending by failure to accept his own logic on the question of immortality, even though he has set it down accurately enough in Grace Severne's chilling soliloquy. He has also failed to accept the artistic logic of the novel, which requires a further development of Alan Vincent as the scientist-hero whose moral flaw has been exposed by the remarkable nature of his scientific discoveries. A man like Alan Vincent thus anticipates the scientist of the 1960s, faced with even greater moral dilemmas in the era of the hydrogen bomb. In the same way, Street should have been further developed, to make the book fully satisfactory as a work of art, since he too looks forward to the new type of man the twentieth century is producing.

These are two of the less satisfactory aspects of *The Elixir of Life*. They reveal that Satchell has here over-extended himself. His lack of complete imaginative grasp of his material is given further emphasis by the various passages of over-writing, and unsatisfactory use of language in other ways.

If further proof were needed that Satchell is writing against the grain of an intuitive understanding of his story's meaning, it is given in a passage early in the book where Philip Westland reflects on the nature of childhood. The garden of childhood is central to Satchell's romantic vision in all his fiction. It connects up his ideas of exile, innocence, and nature. In his next novel, *The Greenstone Door,* the innocence of the childhood experiences of Cedric Tregarthen is set up in contrast to the corruption and disasters of his adult life. Wholeness is the condition of life in the childhood world, which can only be rediscovered during adult life in the garden of nature. This intuition is the basis of Satchell's romanticism.

But what does Philip Westland say in *The Elixir of Life?* "We tell one another that childhood is the time of happiness, but is it? It appears so mainly because, to our adult eyes, it shows beautiful, but as a matter of fact the devil Fear stalks through the garden of childhood and dominates it." This statement, set against the mainstream of Satchell's thinking, reveals his mind groping toward a new view of life, but unsuccessfully. In *The Greenstone Door* he portrays the fairy-tale childhood happiness of the young people, Cedric Tregarthen, Rangiora, and Puhi-Huia, in the New Zealand bush. The devil Fear stalks through this garden, but does not dominate it. The domination of Fear comes in the adult life of the characters in this last, great novel.

A further imaginative failure in *The Elixir of Life* is Satchell's inability to work out properly his ideas on the question of true love, which he so emphatically favored in the Hokianga novels. These views were a part of his Positivist thinking. According to Comte and Feuerbach, true love was the panacea of life, the universal principle. In both the Hokianga novels and in *The Greenstone Door,* Satchell strongly agrees with the Positivists. He believes, with them, that a love of that kind—as experienced by Mrs. Andersen, by Cedric's dead father and mother, by Lena Andersen, and even at the last by Eve Milward—is sanctified by something higher than man-made laws.

The same love is felt by Alan Vincent toward Grace Severne

in *The Elixir of Life*. But why do the estranged Alan and Agnes suddenly reveal to each other that they both intend to contract bigamous marriages—Alan to Grace Severne, Agnes to her wealthy friend in New Zealand? "We shall be in the same boat then, and whatever we do will react upon ourselves." And do Alan and Grace need to get "married" by the Reverend Mr. Bule on the ship? Why should Alan go through with this ceremony when "he knew of a certainty that no form devised by man could bind him to the girl with greater security than his sense of honor and the strength of a natural passion"? He and Grace achieve consummation of their love only through a pretense of legality, which makes a mockery of the religious ceremony, as well as of the noble sentiments about natural passion or true love.

But *The Elixir of Life* does raise large issues about the present and future condition of man. It reveals new aspects of human behavior among people under heavy emotional stress. "Every deed done here in this cabin," Alan Vincent says, "must carry consequences more momentous to mankind . . . than any act of human intelligence since the beginning of the world." Satchell overstates the position, of course, yet *The Elixir of Life* already shows him moving away from the regionalism and local color of the Hokianga novels: regionalism was not enough. In *The Greenstone Door* he shifts his artistic focus to another scene, but still speaks of man's fate in universal terms.

CHAPTER 5

Tragic Hero

J UST as the Hokianga novels had shown the advance of white pioneer society into the romantic country of the gumfield and the bush, so *The Greenstone Door* shows the white man's civilization and military strength overcoming old Maori civilization. And as the gumfields and the bush took their toll in men's lives from among the pioneers, so the Maori tribes take their toll in blood as the price of conquest and uneasy peace. The book contains Satchell's most comprehensive expression of feeling about racial problems in the world, especially about friction in New Zealand as a multi-racial society.

Following the example of Walter Scott's historical novels, Satchell introduced most of the leading people of the Maori Wars as characters. Governor Grey, Bishop Selwyn, and General Cameron appear on the white side; old Waharoa, his son Wiremu Tamihana, chief of the Ngati Haua, and Rewi Maniapoto, chief of the Ngati Maniapoto, are on the Maori side. All except Grey, however, play very minor parts in the narrative.

In order to dramatize the conflict Satchell centered his story on an imaginary white trader, Purcell, who lives in a *pa* (fortified settlement) in Maniapoto territory at "Matakiki" on the Waipa river. It is Purcell's tragedy and his glory that he believes in the Maori cause—he is the spokesman for Satchell's romanticism and for much else in his thought—though he takes no active part in the Maori fighting against white attacks.

The portrait of Purcell is loosely based on the real-life trader Philip Tapsell of Maketu, who took part in the assault on Te Tumu pa in 1836 about the same time as the attack on "Te Kuma" pa at the beginning of the novel. Tapsell's Maori wife was killed in the battle of Orakau, the fight which marked the end of the Waikato War. In the novel, Puhi-Huia, Purcell's half-caste daughter, dies in the same battle, but he and his Maori wife Roma escape during the breakout from the fort. At the end Purcell is captured and executed for selling rifles to the Maori tribesmen.

Purcell is thus more than just one of the "lost" characters of Satchell's Hokianga novels. He is also Satchell's only attempt to portray a tragic hero. The tragedy of the takeover of Maori New Zealand by the British settlers in the nineteenth century is epitomized in Purcell's fate, with all the comment on human nature and the human condition which that fate implies. Purcell is not, however, the actual hero of the novel in the conventional sense. This role is taken by the story's narrator, Cedric Tregarthen, and it is significant that here for the first time in his novels Satchell gives up the third-person form of narration to tell his story in the first person. It is a device which considerably intensifies the emotional tone, though it leads at times to an over-dramatic excess of feeling. But it enables Satchell to maintain Purcell as the novel's tragic hero in the strictly classical meaning of the term.

1 *Paradise of Childhood*

The tragedy of Purcell's life is that he goes against "his kind," the British troops and settlers in New Zealand. More than that he is a social outcast who prefers to live in a Maori *pa* rather than in a white settlement. The colonial capital of Auckland is the focus of civilization, as opposed to Matakiki, the focal point of Maori life. Also living at Matakiki *pa* are two other of the "lost" or doomed characters so typical of a Satchell novel: Rangiora, the young Maori chief, and the girl Puhi-Huia, Purcell's daughter.

As the champion of Maori rights, Purcell is directly opposed by Governor George Grey, who lives at Government House in Auckland and is the supreme representative of society in New Zealand. The link between these two opposed figures is Purcell's adopted son and the story's narrator, Cedric Tregarthen, who spends his childhood in the *pa* at Matakiki and his early manhood in Auckland, where he works at Government House as Grey's private secretary.

It is clear that Satchell has refined and simplified his narrative method in *The Greenstone Door* by making Cedric the story-teller. The powerful unity of effect accomplished by such a first-person narration condenses the spaciousness of the historical framework and tightens the diverse incidents into an emotional wholeness. But the variety created by the shifting narrative viewpoints (including the author's) in the previous novels is lost. Yet the book has a modern flavor insofar as Cedric reflects and observes more than he acts.

The impact of the early pages about Cedric's childhood is powerful, because of the exotic and savage surroundings. But this section also serves Satchell's purpose by showing the conflict between civilization and nature in another sense. The innocent, "natural" behavior of Cedric and his childhood Maori friends is contrasted with the cynicism, expediency, and intrigue which he encounters as a young man in Auckland and in the Governor's household. Childhood too, in Satchell's view, is a part of the lost paradise of mankind, and the ideal childhood, for him, is the one which takes place in the bush and among the Maoris and outcasts who form the wilderness inhabitants of all his novels. Yet if by making Cedric an orphan reared and educated under Purcell's tutelage in the bush Satchell engenders sympathy for his hero, he has also made Cedric's childhood friends, the Maori boy chief Rangiora and Puhi-Huia, too idealized to be fully satisfactory artistic creations. They say too little; they are not presented at sufficient length. Even the childhood episodes of play and adventure, rendered though they are with charm and beauty, are not enough to make Rangiora and Puhi-Huia live before the reader in all the richness they deserve. In a way their death in the Battle of Orakau at the end is a mere dramatic gesture, moving though it is and necessary though it is to the novel's dark theme.

The story is a tragic one for Cedric in more ways than that of Purcell's death. But the tragic note is muted on the last few pages when Cedric is united with Helenora, the beautiful, mischievous woman who is Governor Grey's ward. And Cedric also learns that he has his own rightful place in society on the highest level. Although he lives with the Maoris from the age of three, after old Waharoa has killed his father at Te Kuma, he later discovers from Helenora's mother that he is the descendant of an English lord and the heir to a wealthy estate. But it is too much of a coincidence that Helenora's mother, Lady Wylde, is the lover whom his father threw over when he left England for New Zealand before Cedric was born. Satchell's plots are often too outrageous for us today.

At any rate the values of society triumph finally in Cedric's private life, as they do for Geoffrey Hernshaw and Hugh Clifford. But for him far more than for Hernshaw or Clifford the triumph is a tragic one, since it involves the destruction of all the friends he had grown up with, in the bitter fighting of the Waikato War. Once again the meaning is that "civilization is a ruthless thing. One is tempted to ask if it is worth the cost." Cedric in fact loses his sanity for a while, and lives in a cave in the bush, where Helenora nurses him back to health.

The book lives most bountifully in its wilderness sections. In particular the narrative of Cedric's childhood, which occupies the first third of the story—the first nine chapters and the first hundred odd pages—contains the most beautiful and most moving writing. This is the paradise of childhood which Satchell creates out of pure imagination like a glittering, shadowy microcosm of the real world. But here too he is more guilty of the excesses of romanticism than anywhere else in his novels.

It could be said that to a large extent the romanticism of *The Greenstone Door* marks the end of Satchell's way of writing about New Zealand. Clearly we no longer feel romantic today. Satchell had in fact reached there the end of his imaginative journey. Such a realization, more than external events, may explain why this was his final novel. The first nine chapters contain his most flamboyant expression of what might be called the decadence of romanticism. This manner continued in poetry and fiction long after 1914, notably in the poems of A. R. D. Fairburn; see as well the essays of M. H. Holcroft which begin with *The Deepening Stream* (1940)—the whole decline of romanticism has been analyzed by Kendrick Smithyman in his recent study of New Zealand poetry, *A Way of Saying* (1965). But there was a change in the emotional climate which made it difficult for any succeeding novelist to write of the bush as Satchell had done in *The Greenstone Door*. The anti-romantic in New Zealand fiction of the 1920s and 1930s is dominant, even if the work of such a highly individual writer as Roderick Finlayson stands against the stream.

This decadence of feeling and language, which reached a

peak before World War I, shows for example in the following passage from *The Greenstone Door*. It would be impossible to write about a New Zealand scene in the same fashion today. Though we have no way of judging whether Satchell was imaginatively in tune with the time of events in the story, his prose strikes a false note here.

It was a beautiful morning in the early spring, and as, clear of the pa, we ran gleefully down the well-defined bush track, the morning carol of the bell-birds still pealed among the branches overhead. Flocks of parakeets flew with a whistling chatter from tree to tree, and in the dark boughs of the taraires unnumbered pigeons gobbled the purple fruits. Now and then, with harsh cries, a troop of parrots would whirl upwards into the blue sky and, circling in the air, drop again a mile away into the billowing foliage.[1]

An examination of the language of this passage reveals its falsity, and hence a similar falsity of the feeling, which can be called sentimentalism. Words and phrases like "gleefully," "well-defined," "morning carol," "pealed," "whistling chatter," "unnumbered," "gobbled," "troop," and "billowing" all reveal tired diction and shoddy metaphor. The passage has largely the same kind of effect that one might find in *The Coral Island* by R. M. Ballantyne, and it has about the same kind of appeal.

The infantilism of a word like "gobbled" is repeated in the whole of this chapter (Chapter IV) in various ways. One way is in the childish naming used in the play of the three children, Cedric, Rangiora, and Puhi-Huia.

"You are the Little Finger of Te Waharoa," he resumed . . . and what is the value of a little finger without a body? Dost thou know who I am, pakeha?" "I suspect," I replied . . . "you are Rangiora, the son of the Great One and the Spider's Web."

This is of course a mockery of the metaphorical speech used in classical Maori (the children are speaking in Maori). Again and again that sort of thing occurs.

On another page there is the following:

"The Spider's Web would allow me freedom," said Rangiora, "but the Great One forbids it. My soul is sick with longing for liberty. Even my slaves have more freedom than I. Scarce an hour have I moved unhampered, and behold, they are upon me."

It is certain that Rangiora would not have spoken in this way, and the same criticism applies to the speech of the other two children in this section. The romantic heightening of the language once again falsifies the text. The affectation and sentimentality are undeniable.

Yet such is the charming quality of this childhood section of the novel, that in context the reader's eye is able to pass uncritically over these fancies, accepting them as a kind of archaism suitable to the period. We fall in with the game temporarily, for the sake of the mature, unyielding realism of the anti-romantic sequel in the children's adult life.

2 *Natural Man*

Purcell rescues Cedric from Waharoa and brings him up at Matakiki as his foster-son. In much the same way, Governor Grey considers Helenora his ward. But Purcell is a man of mystery. His past life is never revealed, nor are the reasons for his exile to the remote Maori village explained. He lives among the Maoris as a trader, running his axes, blankets, rifles, tobacco, and other trade goods up the rivers by canoe, after a schooner has brought them from Onehunga to Kawhia Harbor. He marries Roma, a slave girl in the *pa*. He is rebellious, but scholarly and humane, and he passes his learning on to Cedric, whom he loves. His tenderness toward his submissive wife is one of the gentler emotions in the book. But he is also possessed of a mighty compassion, and his vision of mankind, ennobled above the petty racial conflict in which he is trapped, is inspiring. Largely through the strength of his portrait, the world Satchell creates in *The Greenstone Door* is a greater and deeper world than in any other of his novels.

In a way Purcell resembles Magwitch, the sinister but benevolent criminal in Dickens's *Great Expectations,* who is transported to the Australian convict settlements, who pays for young Pip's education, and secretly returns to England a rich man. Satchell was certainly affected by the book. For the big house where Miss Havisham lived in *Great Expectations* Satchell has substituted Government House in Auckland. But Helenora's mother, Lady Wylde, is no Miss Havisham, except that she mourns her dead lover, Cedric's father. Helenora makes Cedric fall in love with her, not quite as Estella did with Pip, but out of misguided thoughts of revenging her mother, and without her mother's urging. There is also some resemblance between Satchell's novel and Robert Louis Stevenson's two Jacobite novels, *Kidnapped* and *Catriona,* where a similar historical situation is used as the basis of similar incidents and characters are described by a first-person narrator, David Balfour, who is rather like Cedric Tregarthen in many ways. Nevertheless, *The Greenstone Door* is an essentially individual work of art.

Cedric is a more satisfactory character than the heroes of Satchell's previous novels, mainly because the section describing his childhood brings him more fully to life. As a young man, however, he is over-virtuous, priggish if highly intelligent, aristocratic in temperament, and an expert boxer—in short an incredibly clean, brave, young gentleman. But his defect in the eyes of Government House society, and his appeal to the reader, is that he loves his Maori friends and the old *pa* life. He is, in the words of the dandyish Captain Wylde, "Helenora's New Zealander," a kind of curious freak from the bush.

It is a typical Satchell contrivance, recalling *The Land of the Lost,* to have Cedric meet Helenora by chance when he falls off his horse on the Onehunga road during his first visit to Auckland. Altogether the sugary nature of the Government House sections of the book—Auckland for instance is called by Cedric "the City of Sweet Memories," for he is supposed to be writing down the events of the story in his old age—is tiresome, as are the passages of historical explanation which Cedric inserts in his narrative (tiresome but needful for most readers at the time of publication).

But if Cedric is natural man who becomes civilized and survives to a mellow and somewhat sentimental old age, then Purcell is civilized man who renounces society for the bush and becomes natural man incarnate. It is curious that before his death he makes a large settlement of money on Cedric from his investments in London. Were these investments the product of his trading business, or were they inherited from some family estate? This is not explained, except by Purcell's remark: "I was not among the poor creatures who created it." Even his Christian name is never spoken in the book.

He remains a gigantic, brooding, mysterious figure, whose moral picturesqueness lies in the impression that there is a guilty secret, a darkness in his past, that insulates him from the rest of mankind, and that he is not untouched with impurity or unacquainted with evil. Yet like Major Milward in *The Toll of the Bush* he lacks a sharp focus; he says too little in the book; he is shown to us too little. Nevertheless the account of his last years and death takes over much of the novel's interest. He is one of those "strong and resolute" men of the pioneering days mentioned in *The Toll of the Bush*—"men who laid hold with two hands, men whose deep chests spoke of mighty organs and the power to achieve great desires by the force of great vitalities." The climax of *The Greenstone Door* is tragic, therefore, because Purcell is destroyed by the civilization he despises—by the law of Government House in Auckland and by the petty revenge of the small men of finance in the city.

The figure of Purcell is created more deeply out of Satchell's moral consciousness than anyone else in his fiction. He is doubtless a key figure in any analysis of Satchell's art, the clearest expression of that impulse which drove Satchell himself into trying to become a frontier settler in the Hokianga bush country. Purcell is the pioneer idealized into an archetype. A giant of huge vitality, tremendous physique, and great courage, an adventurer yet wise and compassionate in all his dealings with others, he is a composite of men like F. E. Maning and John Webster of early Hokianga days, with something extra added. "Whence did he come, and why?" Cedric asks himself. "What tragedy was it that cut one so brilliant off from his kind and thrust him into the arms of savagery? Was it a natural misanthropy?" Cedric decides that "an intellectual impatience with man's social systems might lie at the root of his choice."

One striking thing about Purcell is that he was able to counteract for a time the evil influence at the *pa* of the warlike Te Atua Mangu, the Maori priest or *tohunga* who saw in the coming of the white traders and missionaries a challenge to his old power. It is all a little like Joseph Conrad's Tuan Jim at Patusan, with Te Atua Mangu in the place of the Rajah. Purcell was a civilizing influence, first because his trade brought peace and prosperity to the *pa,* and also because he persuaded the tribe to listen to the missionary Mr. Hall and become Christians. But on Purcell himself, when he goes to the city, the effect is dramatic; he hates the "lumber" of civilization.

Never shall I forget the sight of his giant figure striding down the street one morning in the early spring. "This then is Auckland," he said, and looked neither to the right nor the left . . . "All the old institutions, Cedric. Man can never wipe the slate clean and begin anew. He carries all his lumber with him, good, bad, and indifferent." I could detect the old impatience in his tones.[2]

Later the meeting between Purcell and Governor Grey becomes a direct confrontation of opposing values, in which the issues of civilization versus the wilderness are plainly stated. So Purcell is exultant when Cedric refuses to go to England to live with his grandfather Lord Tregarthen, but prefers instead to return with him to live in the bush. Cedic contrasts the appearance of the two men when they meet in Auckland.

Two prouder men never lived. Neither by his office nor by nature was the Governor fitted to take a subservient part; on the other hand, I could not conceive my father bending his kingly head in humility to any office or man . . . The minds of the two men were evidently in sympathy, but the physical contrast between them forced itself strongly on my notice. Sir George, slender, upright, finely proportioned; my father, huge and rugged, and with a slouch forward of the head which came of dwelling in habitations too small for him. None would have been likely to guess the man of learning in the latter. A poet of nature, perhaps, a thinker, but scarcely a scholar. There were moments, on the other hand, and this was one of them, when it was difficult to think of the Governor as a soldier and a man of action; when he seemed, on the contrary, born and fitted for the life of a student. Beyond a glance as I entered the room, they took no notice of me. . . . [3]

In a similar way Purcell brings Cedric back to a nobler view of racial matters: "I am colour-blind . . . There was a time in the history of this planet when the white man was the savage and the swarthy man the person of intellect. It will come again. To be white will not then seem so admirable even to the white

man." Once when Cedric asks him: "To what race do you belong, father?" "To the human race, my son," is his answer.

When Cedric learns that Purcell has been supplying arms to
the rebellious Maoris, he sadly thinks: "What a splendid tolerance was his, but for that one fatal exception—civilization! And
now it had carried him—how far?" He sees that Purcell has committed himself irrevocably to the anti-social forces that had first
driven him into the wilderness, and he knows that his foster-
father is therefore doomed: "Despair was in my heart . . . The
solid earth seemed to have slipped from beneath, leaving me in
some land of nightmare. Impassable barriers encompassed me.
Look where I would, no road revealed itself." Cedric thus discovers that life outside society in opposition to civilization must
lead to anarchy, chaos, and death, and that there is "no road"
back for men so committed as Purcell to the primitive, natural
world.

Just as classical tragedy revolves about heroes of great nobility, in actions of the broadest magnitude, so the protagonists and
events in *The Greenstone Door* are large. Sir George Grey, New
Zealand's great colonial statesman and British Governor in the
Maori Wars, is opposed in Purcell by a mysterious, noble English exile, in every human way his equal. Satchell has emphasized
the importance of the actors in his novel just as a classical tra-
gedian does, to give his audience a sense of the highest human
significance of the drama. Like all tragedies, *The Greenstone
Door* induces universal sympathy for its hero by the established
method of the recognition scene near its end. Following his court
martial by the British troops, Purcell consciously recognizes his
own tragic flaw—it is "bad citizenship"—and gloriously con-
fronts his fate without flinching and without regret, in the following scene with Cedric.

"It is well that our friend Bacon chose to glorify action rather than
being," he said; "for according to the philosophy of Plato he would
have made but a poor showing."

"Oh, father!" I cried, taking his hand and holding it between my
own, "talk not to me of books; tell me only how I may save your
life."

"You cannot, my son," he said gravely. "There is no way unless
Brompart relents; and even then it is but to defer the end."

"Why should he desire your death? When he robbed you, why did you not prosecute him?"

"Ah, why! It was bad citizenship."

"Father, if you have no care for your life, have compassion on my misery. Tell me what I can do."

"Life is no less desirable to me than to other men," he said, "but I recognise the inevitable when I am in front of it. There is a fire in this man's heart that nothing we can do will quench. Be at peace, my son. It is but to forestall by a few years an inevitable natural event. Come, let me hear your adventures." [4]

Such a recognition by a tragic hero of the true nature of existence, of the reasons for his fate and the necessity of his involvement and sacrifice in the great human struggle, is one of the distinguishing marks of tragedy. Purcell recognizes his weakness, his inability to accept civilization and its responsibilities of good citizenship, and so is able to go to his death in front of a firing squad in full knowledge of his failure, and at peace with the world.

3 *The Road and the Door*

Satchell was the first man to write with eloquence and genuine understanding of brown New Zealand. In places *The Greenstone Door* burns with a fiery, controlled anger against the hatred and contempt expressed by many early British settlers in New Zealand for the Maoris. He exposes in it the hypocrisy of many of the minor missionaries, land speculators, and small businessmen, who exploited the Maoris or failed to understand them. In exhuming this conflict his imagination works vividly in terms of two dominant images—the images of the road and the door.

His picture of old Maori *pa* life, based on such good studies as *The Maori Race* by Edward Tregear, is highly colored. Yet in many ways the opening section of the novel, describing Cedric's childhood in the *pa*, is the most exciting and readable, despite its exaggerations. It is full of tenderness, humor, and clear scene-painting. On the first pages, Cedric's account of himself hidden in the fern—that most evocative experience of a New Zealand childhood—leads immediately and with only a slight straining for effect, to his description of Waharoa's war-party attacking Te Kuma.

Around me, tangling its fronds above my head, is high fern, shutting out the hot rays of the March sun. There are strange creatures moving on the soil, whizzing past among the leaves. . . . I push my way on and on, following the black cicadas and brown locusts, as they leap before me. . . . There is a sound in the air, slowly detaching itself from the silence; a booming, hollow sound, a rhythmic sound, swelling and falling. . . I can see the war-party heartening itself for the attack, the rhythmic stamping of feet, the rolling eyes, the horrible grimaces; I can hear the threatening staccato of the war-song, the voice of the leader, the guttural response of the taua, as a fire crackling from lip to lip, the fierce shout, the deep, blood-curdling gasp, filling the air with a whisper of death—"Hi! Hi! Ha-ah!" [5]

The account of the three children playing in the fern later on as Cedric grows up in the Maori *pa*—the tale of the secret tunnel through the fern, and the hidden rock staircase down into the Waipa river gorge—is full of delight. The limestone cave by the river with its stalactites and stalagmites shaped like human figures, and the limestone curtain on which appears as on a frieze a picture in stone of the tragic events to come, is one of Satchell's most original and magical inventions. Although Cedric and Rangiora argue angrily over the relative rights of whites and Maoris to live in New Zealand, a change occurs in their relationship when Rangiora saves Cedric from drowning in the river. That is when the two make their childish compact of the title phrase—the "greenstone door" compact of truce between them. Writing down the story seventy years later, Cedric records Rangiora's statement as follows:

"Little Finger," he said softly, "let that talk die between us for ever. In the hour that I found you in the water my eyes were opened, and I saw how deep the plant of friendship had rooted itself in my heart. Had you died then, to me also death had been welcome. So it is with me. I pray that it may be so with you also." His musical voice had taken on a bewitching charm, and for a moment my eyes were dim, so that I could scarcely see him. "Let us forget that we are of two races," he continued, "and remember that we are also of one—the race of mankind. Never shall my hand be raised against you and yours. Let not your hand be lifted against me and mine. Let us rather make between us the compact of the Tatau Pounamu, and if in the years to come one of us should reopen that which is shut, on his head be the loss and the shame. Behold, the Greenstone Door is closed."

"It is closed," said I.[6]

Satchell's use of the greenstone door image in this scene (the phrase is a translation of a metaphorical ancient Maori expression, as the above quotation shows—*tatau pounamu,* which means enduring peace) is later given an ironic reversal, at the end, in his characteristic manner. The children who make the peace pact between white man and brown man live to see it broken when they grow to manhood, and then tragically "sealed in blood" when Rangiora and Puhi-Huia are killed at the Battle of Orakau.

Even so, Satchell's use of the phrase does not exactly agree with Maori tradition. Thus there is no exchange of gifts between Cedric and Rangiora as usually marked the speaking of the metaphor in ancient Maori usage. The giving of the greenstone—generally a greenstone (or jade) war-club or some other valuable article—occurred most often after a tribal battle or personal duel, just as Rangiora's speech marked the end of their quarrel over the relative merits of whites and Maoris. Moreover the gift of greenstone was in the nature of opening a gateway to peace rather than closing a door on war. However, this is a minor point, for Satchell maintains the spirit of the metaphor throughout the book, even though he uses it unsuitably to mark the end of the quarrel also between the Tregarthen and Wylde families, when in the novel's last sentence Cedric, reunited with Helenora, says that for them too the greenstone door is closed— or as he more explicitly wrote in his manuscript before he made his final corrections in proof: "So between your house and mine there is peace—the peace of the Greenstone Door. The past is dead and forgotten. The door is closed and before us lies the future. Will it make amends?" [7]

The metaphor is well documented in such studies of Maori life as Elsdon Best's *Tuhoe.* Soon after the battle of Orona in 1822 between the Tuhoe and Taupo tribes, Best says, "an abiding peace was made between the two peoples. The *tatau pounamu* (jade door) which bars war and strife, was set up at Opepe on the Taupo-Napier Road." Best also records that at the

end of the Hau Hau War, Major Mair met Te Whenua-nui and
others of Tuhoe at Te Umu-o-Kaiawa, Ruatoki, on September 25,
1870, where the Maoris "submitted and cried enough." As a
token of their being in earnest, and to bind the peace, two
greenstone weapons (one of which was named Tuhua) and
three Maori cloaks were handed over to the government representative. In return, Mair gave the Maoris a watch, a gold pin,
a gold ring, and a shawl. "The watch was named Maunga-rongo
(peace-making)."

Satchell's creative imagination worked unobtrusively but deeply, and to some extent Cedric, as the bearer of the pact with
Rangiora between white man and brown, becomes himself the
"greenstone door" or gift of valuable qualities from the Maoris
to the white settlers—that is, the peacemaker. This is notably
so in his work of explaining Maori culture to Governor Grey
during his years as Grey's private secretary, and on his journey-
ings with Grey and Bishop Selwyn to visit Maori villages in the
bush before war breaks out. Also when the war does start, he is
employed as a peacemaker between the two factions by both
Grey and Purcell, and finally is given papers appointing him
official interpreter to General Cameron, who is in charge of the
British troops in the war.

In other ways the image of the door recurs in the novel. Thus
when Purcell wishes to set up a second trading post in the Maori
tribal territory of Huata, chief of Kawhia, he is seen as opening
a door of peace by exchanging trade goods for greenstone.
Huata, the *ariki* or chief, questions Te Moanaroa:

"Does the white man seek to open a doorway for his tribe?" the
ariki asked, fixing his fierce, dark eyes on Purcell.

"No, but for the treasures of the white man's country," responded
Te Moanaroa. "Guns are good and the things of iron—axes and
knives . . . Even I myself have paid much good greenstone for
tobacco." [8]

So Huata agrees to have a "compact" with Purcell, and this is a
doorway of peace too, because the trade goods bring prosperity:

The age of the musket had passed away. Cattle and horses, agricultural implements and seed were now the things dear to and desired
of the chiefs . . . A profound peace—the first for centuries—had set-

tled on the land. The people had advanced sufficiently far into civilisation to perceive its grandeur and beauty, yet not so far that they
had lost confidence in themselves and their possibilities. An enthusiasm had sprung up for the things and ideas of the white people.

But it is a special kind of peace, for no other white men are
permitted to enter the territory of Huata:

Item by item the trader's demands were debated and upheld. White
men had deceived them in the past, but this was a man alone. What
he said came to pass.

The moral nature of the conflict between civilization and the
bush is given explicit prominence in the book. A tone of Swiftian
satire is achieved during Cedric's first visit to Auckland; the
rough behavior and language of the seamen on the schooner
that takes him to Onehunga causes him to reflect: "If this were
civilization then give me savagery." Even the "cultivated tongue"
of Purcell's business agent in Auckland, a land speculator named
William Brompart, contains sinister implications that look forward to Brompart's sons' betrayal of Purcell during the war.
"Mr. Brompart spoke in rapid jerks, seldom taking the trouble to
finish his sentences, but completing his meaning with sharp
movements of the head and a cocking of his queer, shrewd
eyes."
     Governor Grey, who is with Helenora when Cedric is thrown
off his horse a few pages later, says: "Property . . . that is the
secret of civilization. The first man who possessed himself of a
stick started on a path to the stars." So the reader is prepared
for the war against the Maoris, which was caused by the white
settlers' insatiable desire for Maori lands. A further doubt about
the moral value of civilization is raised in Cedric's mind by the
attitude of the townsfolk toward the Maoris living in Auckland,
which was

. . . at the best tolerance, at the worst a scurrilous contempt that
enveloped the whole native race in the epithet "bloody Maoris."
     I am not now speaking of those hardy and courageous settlers,
true chips of the ancient Anglo-Saxon block, who, taking their lives
in their hands, had gone forth into the wilderness, there to hew out
for themselves the homes the old land denied them—they, at least,

were compelled by their necessities to hold the original owners of the soil in respect; nor of the men of culture and understanding who were able to pierce the dark skin of ignorance and observe with admiration the natural strength of brain beneath; but of the mass of the townsmen, themselves of no particular education, of narrow, insular views and absorbed in the petty issues of trade.[9]

The effect of the white man's civilization on the Maoris themselves was equally bad, after what Cedric had known of them as a child:

I had been accustomed to dignity and reserve, to courteous speech, to honourable dealing; here I could see little of any of them. The men were boisterous and tricky, the women bold and worse. . . . He who came with a boisterous jest found a boisterous jester to receive him. The speech underlined with senseless oaths was responded to in like fashion.

However, Cedric's outlook on life becomes tainted too by white society's values. When he returns to Matakiki during the absence of Grey and the Wyldes in England, he says to Rangiora, using the familiar Satchell image of the road: "But this is a new age, Rangiora. It lies along the road of the white man and not the ancient track of the Maori." He is also jealous of Rangiora's love for Puhi-Huia, who looks and behaves more like a white girl than a halfcaste.

It was natural with one brought up as I had been that colour should not assume that immense importance it has in the eyes of the ordinary white man; yet it was there, a creation of my three years in Auckland. But far more potent than this in giving me a vague sense of dissatisfaction and uneasiness was the new-born knowledge of the disparity that existed between the inheritor of civilisation and the child of savage parents.[10]

The outbreak of war causes the pioneer settlers in the bush to quit Maori territory, and "all roads" are "closed against the white man." With regret Cedric now comes to realize that "the road to peace ran through the iron gateway of war"—not through the greenstone doorway of love such as had existed between him and Rangiora, nor through the door of trade and prosperity which existed between Purcell and the Ngatimaniapoto.

The road image recurs frequently in the last part of the book. The tracks of the Maoris lead in circles or into impenetrable bush when Cedric is seeking a way through to save his foster-father. Conversely the military road of the white soldiers, which he must avoid, goes in a broad, inexorable movement forward. Even when Cedric gallops off on a horse to get a reprieve for his foster-father from General Cameron, after young Brompart has sentenced him to be shot following the mockery of a court martial, he is again defeated by the bush: "on a made road however poor its condition, it would have been an easy feat; but for two thirds of the distance the way was but a narrow track."

The image of the wrong door—the door of war and hate instead of peace and love—also recurs when Cedric is locked in a wooden hut by the Maoris to stop him from persuading Purcell to come back to the white side in the conflict: "This door had escaped any special observation till the sound of heavy bars falling into place directed my attention to its size and strength." While he spends eight months in this captivity, gradually the enchanted Maori world of his childhood turns into the tragic prison of his manhood. When finally he gets back to General Cameron's troops to work as an interpreter and peacemaker, he meets Rangiora for the last time at Orakau fort.

He must have recognised me the instant I appeared beyond the palisade, but now for the first time he gazed steadily upon me. "Little Finger," he replied, wiping a trickle of blood from his lips—and in his voice was the old, magical sweetness—"you and I sought to close the Greenstone Door with a bond of love—that will always remain to us in our honour; but it is in blood that the sealing will be done. But let be. Those words that have passed between us are for always; this word that divides us is but for a little time. Now go, my brother, for we have chosen." [11]

This pitiful ending to the dream of love and friendship created during Cedric's childhood is followed immediately by the terrible court martial sequence. Here again love between members of the two races has a disastrous ending when Purcell's Maori wife, Roma, unknowingly condemns him to death out of her own mouth, in one of the most moving scenes in New Zealand fiction.

"In short, your husband was associated with the natives in their resistance to the Queen's troops," continued the inquisitor; "he sat in their councils and participated in their battles?"

"Why not?" asked Roma, rising to her feet, and looking round the faces at the table, as though for the first time the significance of the proceedings had come home to her. "He is a chief of the Ngatima-niapoto."

It was an unfortunate defence, and I knew by the sudden glitter in Brompart's eyes and the slight movement of the others that its effect was far other than the unhappy woman had contemplated.[12]

So the door of love also fails Purcell in the distortion of values created by the inter-racial conflict. The door and the road are key images in this as in all Satchell's fiction. But here it is a military road, and as such it is evil.

4   *Good and Evil*

Beneath the conflict between civilization and the wilderness, and beneath the racial conflict, there is a further struggle being fought in *The Greenstone Door*. This is the battle between good and evil, which is brought out in certain sections of the book. In particular Chapter VII, titled "The War of Light and Darkness," shows how Maori "witchcraft" defeats the Christian "message of love" which the missionaries bring to the bush.

When the missionary Mr. Hall visits the *pa* of Huata and is put to a test of strength by the Maoris, he pompously says: "In the hands of the Lord evil itself becomes an instrument for good." But the *pa* of Huata is filled with evil omens, such as the red-ochred death houses, the obscene, emaciated, female undertaker, the decaying heads of decapitated enemies on the poles of the palisades, the locked armory full of guns, and finally the Maori *tohunga*, Te Atua Mangu himself—the priest or wizard with a withered, claw-like foot, who casts an evil spell on a boy who mocks him. This boy grows up to become an idiot man who, hypnotized by the *tohunga*, is Cedric's jailer during his captivity and his relentless pursuer when he escapes.

In Satchell's mind the influence of the old *tohunga* was due to a malign, supernatural power that was inhuman, evil, and directly opposed to the white man's Christianity. There is no historical evidence to support this view. But Satchell's sense of evil is a factor in all his novels, and here it becomes a frightening overwhelming force. Such is the motivation behind the scene where the *tohunga* makes green leaves appear on a dead tree during his confrontation with the missionary at the *pa*—an act of "witchcraft" that defeats Mr. Hall's attempt to bring the Gospel to the tribe, since he can perform no similar miracle.

Mr. Hall is depicted in an ironic, mocking way. His bald head and his inability to speak the Maori language properly are made fun of by Cedric. His age, weakness, and ignorance of Maori ways are stressed so as to indicate reasons for the failure of his "message of love"; and his plea for "light" instead of "darkness," or old Maori religion, is seen as almost farcical.

Later on Christianity is accepted by the tribe. Missions and schools are established and there is "an unappeasable demand for Bibles." But that initial defeat is important in the story, for when war breaks out, even Bishop Selwyn admits that Christianity was not enough: "They have logical minds. I have preached the doctrines of Christ, and the followers of Christ come against them with fire and sword." The leaders of the two main tribes in the Waikato and Waipa valleys, Wiremu Tamihana and Rewi Maniapoto, were both devout Christians, and they used the Bible to justify their cause in the war. But as Cedric points out to Wiremu Tamihana during his captivity: "It is to the New Testament you should look, Tamihana, and not to the Old. There you will find little of kings, but much of peace and goodwill." Nevertheless, Tamihana sets up a puppet Maori king from among the chiefs supporting him, to act as a figurehead in opposition to the British Queen Victoria, in whose name the British troops and settlers were fighting.

The big chief Te Huata is a careful portrait by Satchell of an old-time Maori. Externally he resembles paintings that have survived of chiefs of those days:

Though his skin was fairer than that of the generality of his race, his face was so heavily lined with the scrolls of the tohunga-ta's chisel as to appear at a distance almost blue-black. His thick hair was drawn through a ring and, being again caught thereunder, formed a large knot or pad on the crown of his head. His eyes were small, fierce, and rat-like, and there was something also of the rat in the fang-like character of his eye-teeth, which gleamed forth on any quick movement of his mouth. For the rest, he was a man of great stature and apparently huge strength.[13]

Internally, however, he is shown as the most primitive type of savage, and here Satchell's imagination has carried him too far in his striving for a dramatic contrast. Huata is the least credible of the Maoris created in Satchell's fiction and is close to a caricature. Yet there is no doubt as to the power of the drawing, or to the sense of evil in it.

Exasperated to the verge of insanity, his slow mind moved cloudily through the darkness, seeking some way back which might be seductive to his people. He hated the cold, white glare that came over life with the advent of the pakeha. He hated the never-to-be-entirely-dismissed feeling of inferiority to the white-faced interloper. Oh for the comfortable old days when no doubt and unrest disturbed the well-ordered lives! Oh for the return of the time when every autumn brought the excitement of war, the glories of the stricken field, with its flaming whares and multitudinous dead! [14]

However, the scene in which a slave girl is sacrificed and cooked for a ceremonial feast at the old chief's command is a piece of sensationalism. "I remain with my forefathers; their gods suffice me; I will maintain their customs. Away with it! To the priests the heart! Let the ovens be made ready!" Such statements by Huata do not stand up to close scrutiny, either as credible human behavior in the situation described in the book, or in the light of present knowledge of ancient Maori behavior.

In similar fashion, regrettably, the portrait of the old priest Atua Mangu is caricatured. The claw-footed *tohunga* is more a product of fantasy than of real life, a stereotyped personification of evil and viciousness. These aspects of the novel are part of the dark, unpleasant side of Satchell. There is a streak of gloomy despair and pessimism running through *The Greenstone Door,* which shows, if nothing else, how deeply he was affected by the morbidness of nineteenth-century German Romanticism and all its excesses of feeling.

To the extent that the incidents of the curse put on the Maori youth who becomes an idiot, and the bringing of the dead tree to life, are unbelievable they form blemishes in the novel.

Nevertheless, this section of the book is given ambiguity by Satchell's presentation of the incidents as seen through the eyes of Cedric, a boy in his early adolescence, and by the covertly placed suggestion that the *tohunga* has temporarily hypnotized him too. But the latter impression again is negated by the implication that the *tohunga* had supernatural powers which enabled him to turn a normal if cheeky young Maori boy into an idiot.

The power of the *tohunga* is most important during Cedric's imprisonment. But Satchell re-emphasizes it before that, when young Rangiora has to go through his initiation rites before attaining his chieftainship. The supreme rite is the casting of a "death spell" on another member of the tribe. This evil deed Rangiora refuses to do, partly because he has been influenced by Cedric's ideas, but mainly out of his own humane idealism which transcends his desire for power. He does not know that the order to cast the death spell is only a move in a cunning conflict between the *tohunga* and the other Maori leaders, particularly Rangiora's father, in his efforts to bring about war with the white settlers.

The victory of evil is also made clear through the triumph of Fred Brompart, who orders Purcell's execution after the court martial. The Bromparts, land speculators and embezzlers, are representatives of the dishonest commercial dealers and businessmen who for their own gain forced the issue to open war on the settlers' side. Fred Brompart is a reincarnation of the darker nature of Arthur Roller, the fat, arrogant storekeeper in *The Land of the Lost*. Both men represent the "ancient evils" of society. But it is interesting to see how Satchell's mind in *The Greenstone Door* is working in more absolute terms than before. Whereas Arthur Roller had some redeeming features—he was a "good businessman"—Fred Brompart is pure evil: he is "a monster," "a fiend."

The book as a whole does contain a crushing and poignant atmosphere of evil triumphant, and the melancholy side of Satchell's imagination prevails over his high-spirited wittiness and tenderness. But the ordeals of his characters reveal a general moral crisis in society at this stage of human development; it is one which has universal implications even today. That is why the earlier optimism, which in the Hokianga novels, was not altogether consistent either, is all gone in *The Greenstone Door*, despite the conventional happy ending for Cedric and Helenora in each other's arms.

Satchell's revelation and condemnation of unpalatable general truths about human nature was brought about by his long brooding on the tragedy of the Maori Wars of the 1860s and '70s; not only because of the land confiscations which followed, but because of the emotional defeatism which persisted for nearly a century among the Maoris. He used the war situation to illuminate his vision of life in the same way that Tolstoy used the Napoleonic Wars, though Satchell's presentation is on an understandably small scale.

One technical problem that Satchell overcame rather clumsily in *The Greenstone Door* was that of handling the passage of time, with which he also had difficulty in *The Toll of the Bush*. Maybe this roughness of technique is not intrusive except at the point where Cedric leaves Matakiki to visit Grey in Auckland as a peacemaker for the Maoris, when the country is on the edge of war but fighting has not actually broken out. Again he is thrown off his horse, before he reaches Auckland, and he takes several months to recover from an unspecified injury in an unnamed place. This device allows the war to begin and advance to the date of the Oakura massacre in the Taranaki campaign. By that time, of course, it is too late for Cedric to do anything about stopping the war.

Cedric's eight months of imprisonment in the wooden hut at Ngaruawahia, where he meets Wiremu Tamihana, is also an obvious method of passing over a further early period of the fighting, to advance the story rapidly to its climax at Orakau, the final battle of the Waikato campaign which had begun almost a year earlier. On other pages too, three years or five years are passed over in a sentence or two but not always in a satisfying way. The treatment of events is generally rather impressionistic, but accuracy is never sacrificed for the sake of the story.

The use of archaisms emphasizes the period of the novel. For instance, "foretime," "ere," "bourne," "naught," "haled," and similar words are not those which Satchell would normally use. They are introduced in much the same way that he uses vernacular speech in the Hokianga novels.

It is impossible to deny the monumental quality of *The Green-stone Door*. As a novel it has inspired an increasing school of imitators, and innumerable borrowings among modern New Zealand writers, while its handling of the racial question is entirely in line with modern thinking on the subject. Its real power, however, lies in Satchells clearly transmitted feeling that the remedy for the evils he described lay in a change in the spirit of society rather than its form. He got down in his thinking and his art to the basic essence of all human activity, so that the ambiguous moral tone of his colonial community is seen to reflect that of society in general.

CHAPTER 6

Nature and Man

L IKE most early New Zealand writers, William Satchell was
heir in exile to the romantic movement in world literature.
But his youthful interest in haunted abbeys and crumbling castles was superseded after his emigration to New Zealand, even
if the old gothic meanings still pervade so late a work as *The
Greenstone Door*, in his account of life in the *pa* of Te Huata.
His love affair with the virgin New Zealand bush never died out.
Yet the purest expression of his thought is in portraits of exiles
like Purcell. It recurs also in his portrait of the young chief
Rangiora as the type of noble savage whom Rousseau had
thought to exist in the Pacific Islands.

He was a well-proportioned lad, broad in the chest, slender and lithe
at the hips, and carrying himself with a quiet dignity which impressed
me. His hair had been carefully dressed, and was decorated with two
tail feathers of the huia bird. No tattoo marks disfigured the clear
bronze of his skin, which, save for a belt and maro of embroidered
flax, was uncovered by clothing. On his breast hung a valuable jade
jewel of high antiquity, and a light spear of red tea-tree wood was
poised in his right hand.[1]

Thus not only Satchell's fervent response to nature, but his
idealization of those who lived and died in the wilderness, was
decisive in his vision. His wistful memory of his first years in
the romantic Hokianga bush country so absorbed him throughout the fifty remaining years of his life after he left Hokianga
that he was unable to write about contemporary city life, even
though he lived for forty of those fifty years in the city of Auckland. "Nature was in a gentle mood," in early New Zealand, he
wrote, but the settler from Britain and Europe brought "those
ancient evils from which his ancient civilization has never had
the wit to release him." These evils destroyed the balance of nature and brought unwanted conflicts in the pioneer period.

o that of Jessamine Olive at the end of

ond the settlement—a look of inspiration in his
e orchards and the vineyards of the future," he
voices of the children at play among the thick-
the mothers singing at their work. Over all the
ce of God." [2]

knew from bitter experience that this was no
ision; hence the pessimism of his later work. Yet
phasizes, if emphasis were necessary, the strongly
an quality of Satchell's romanticism. Jessamine Olive
ne of Wordsworth's simple but wise peasants. And
ements of Jess's inspiration—and Satchell's, one can
re inhabited by this kind peasantry, they are also
form. The benevolent despot Doctor Hamilton in *The
the Lost* is a preliminary portrait of Major Milward
Toll of the Bush, a more forceful despot whose ledger
ls many lives, and who takes a horsewhip to a defaulter
Fletcher. Milward resembles a feudal lord. Purcell too is
e same feudal breed, in the rule he has over the Maoris in the
pa Valley and Kawhia districts, established by his chain of
ding posts. But it is notable that he and Milward are less
ordsworthian in their opposition to Christianity.

The influence of Wordsworth on Satchell's thought is potent
and undeniable, however, as it is undeniable in many later New
Zealand writers. His dislike of city life is another example of
this kinship: his thought stops short of the city and cannot enter
except with irony and with brevity, as in Chapter XXVII of
The Toll of the Bush, or with sentimentality and distaste as in
the Auckland chapters of *The Greenstone Door.* He sees man
most clearly, as Wordsworth does, in a state of isolation or exile,
behaving most splendidly when closest to nature.

1 *The Other Tenth*

Any attempt to explain the change in Satchell's thought from
the qualified optimism of the Hokianga novels to the pessimism
of *The Greenstone Door* must refer back to his sense of un-

The logic
must pre
simisn
pett,
ness, a
relations
of his pr
vance"—bu
ple orchards a
and children at
Rousseauan ideal
icies adopted by ma
today, while his strict
morality made by later

The brooding, reflectiv
his work its meditative qu
buoyant, gay fancy which pro
light and charm us. Neverthel
toughness of his thinking which
used to describe Purcell might w
"Where might I look for anything his
communicated to mine? He was inter
leaf, the blight upon it, the stone, the sta
sage to him." Satchell too, with his prob
was "interested in everything," but his majo
real study, was man himself. His concept of ma
of his youthful reading of German poets and ph
his actual observations of men and women living i
settlements of the New Zealand bush. His acceptance
science in Darwin and Huxley fought with a Christi
merging into pantheism.

His ideal community existed in the Maori settlements
after Purcell and the missionaries had banished tribal warfa

. . . the halycon time of the race . . . the valleys of the Waipa and
the Waikato became great gardens and granaries . . . the huddled
cultivations at the feet of the pas had spread out into great areas
gilded over with wheat . . . cattle and horses, agricultural implements
and seed were now the things dear to and desired of the chiefs.

[*138*]

It is a similar vision
The Land of the Los
He turns his face be
eyes. "I see the app
says . . . "I hear th
leafed trees. I hea
land rests the pea

But Satchel
more than a
the vision er
Wordsworth
resembles
if the sett
assume—
feudal i
Land o
in *The*
contr
like
of th
Wa
tra

Christian evil in such a story as "'The Man Who Went North,'" or of the perversion of Christianity in a story like "A Martyr to Circumstantial Evidence." In these early novels and stories Satchell's pessimism found powerful but subsidiary expression in his gallery of "the lost." His doomed or demented dwellers of the gumfield and the bush—men like Bart, Jessamine Olive, Sven Andersen, and Mark Gird, who are condemned to death or madness—are also smaller versions of Purcell, the archetype of natural man.

The moral passion of Purcell is admirable; he speaks for mankind and transcends society—"what a splendid tolerance was his." It is not surprising that society destroys him: the old evils still operate even in the clean, bright, New Zealand sunlight. Yet society has gained nothing; it is a petty act of revenge, and Purcell remains the moral victor after the ritual act of shooting him is done.

Purcell illustrates the supreme virtue of living according to one's own view of things, no matter how high the cost. But in the eyes of ordinary people he is a fool who has thrown away his life for an ideal that nobody can properly understand. He is the prototype of the individualist, the "man alone" of the old Maori chief Huata's phrase, the natural man who will not be tamed by the "giant forces of nature" or the "petty conventions" of mankind. His original can be found in the American frontiersmen from Daniel Boone to Davy Crockett, and in men of the New Zealand pioneer period like Dicky Barrett, Philip Tapsell, or John Webster. But he transcends history and becomes larger than life by his "mistake" of siding with the Maoris during the pioneer wars. His death is the nadir of Satchell's pessimism.

Satchell's sympathy with his social outcasts was understandably strong. Most of these men were not native-born New Zealanders (the word "native" in Satchell's day meant a Maori) but came originally from Britain. They were a part of what Satchell called in *The Elixir of Life* "the other tenth." This important phrase in his thinking, as it relates to colonial life, occurs when Philip Westland asks Dr. Alan Vincent what are the motives actuating the immigrants on the ship, "in each case strong enough to overcome the natural dislike of transplantation." Alan replies:

Nine-tenths of them, no doubt, are actuated by the hope that they
may better themselves in a new land; and so the majority of them
will, but not, perhaps, in the way they imagine, or without a period
of misery before their roots take hold in the new soil. The navvies,
for instance, every man of them, will hate New Zealand with a mortal
hatred for the next three or four years, and the older they are the
more intense will be their hatred and the longer it will last.

Then the average working immigrant, Alan believes, will

. . . complain of the climate, the food, the cost of living, the people,
the methods of work—even the labour laws, which were framed for
him alone, and have no parallel in the world. But after that he will
begin to take root, and then New Zealand will be "God's own country"
to him, and he will be a New Zealander.[3]

Philip Westland next asks, "What about the other tenth?" "The
other tenth," Alan replies, "consists of those who are fleeing
from the wrath to come. . . . Buoyed up with a vain hope . . .
more than likely. Tragedy in their hearts . . . Ah, the other
tenth!"

But in *The Greenstone Door* the other tenth of New Zealand's
population are the Maoris, who in the early days were believed
to be a dying race, doomed to extinction. It was the "tragedy"
of this group which caused his pessimistic mood to dominate
this last novel. Moreover he considered their fate to be a sin
against humanity, committed by the white settlers in taking over
the country. He himself did not believe them to be doomed,
but, appalled at the effect on them of the "evils" of the white
man's civilization, he incorporated his feelings into the pages of
The Greenstone Door and in particular into his portrait of the
man Purcell, adopted chief of the Maniapoto. In all his fiction,
in fact, his pessimistic mood is largely related to the loss of
this "other tenth" of society. He believes that these people, often
the noblest and the best, should not be wasted.

2   *The Implacable Fates*

The strain of fatalism in Satchell's work is plainly apparent
in a phrase from the passage just quoted: "the wrath to come."
The "other tenth" flee with a vain hope of survival; their fate

is certain to be tragic. Satchell believed in the survival of
civilized man, but his vision of the irony of much human suffering and striving, as he saw it in Hokianga County in 1890,
sometimes combined with the darker moods of his temperament
to cause him to despair of universal happiness. His thinking
therefore fluctuates between optimism and pessimism in violent
surges of feeling.

An early expression of his fatalism is put into the mouth of
one of his depraved characters, Cuthbert Upmore, proprietor
of the "Scarlet Man" bush pub in *The Land of the Lost*. Upmore is the half brother of Hugh Clifford and his rival for the
inheritance of their father's estate in England, though neither
of them knows it at the time of their first meeting on the edge
of the gumfield. When Upmore sees Clifford approaching the
pub he imagines that he is "the irresponsible instrument of
something hateful behind." The author then interpolates:

A less superstitious man might have taken steps to avoid an encounter
with the traveller; to Upmore's mind this would have been merely
working on the side of destiny. The correct attitude was that of an
automaton, to be set going, shifted about, and stopped at the pleasure
of its maker.

Satchell's irony here shows his condemnation of such views: he
disassociates himself from Upmore's fatalism and from his mech-
anistic view of the universe. He also, by implication, dissociates
himself as the author from Upmore's next reflection when he
sees Clifford approach even closer: "Could this handsome, in-
nocent-looking creature be the messenger of the Implacable
Fates?" Upmore of course is a doomed or "lost" figure.

Satchell thus recognizes the existence of the mythical Fates
only insofar as they rule the lives of men already doomed, that
is, the "other tenth" whose past mistakes have already condemned them. His dislike of the mechanistic-scientific view of
the universe was a natural product of his romanticism. He had
expressed it more explicitly in his ironical poem, "A Scientific
Sing-Song", which ran:

We're all automata, everyone,
We're conscious of nothing until it's done;

The hue of the rose, be it ever so red,
Is naught but the whirl of a wheel in the head.
We're self-adjusting mechanical toys
That weep mechanical pearls,
We're only strong mechanical boys
And sweet mechanical girls.

In *The Toll of the Bush* it looks odd at first sight that Geoffrey Hernshaw should be infected with a view of life similar to Upmore's. But Geoffrey's fatalism is a lesser strain in his personality, brought about by despair and defeat in his personal relationships. Thus when Eve rejects Geoffrey's offer of his love, and old Major Milward urges him to be more firm with her, he thinks:

The "strong grasp" and now the "direct path". . . . Was it not all a delusion that man possessed a free choice in his actions, that he determined them for himself and so hour by hour framed his life? What choice had the moon whether she should circle round the earth, the seed where it should grow, the man if he should be born? Did not the idea of free will in a creature so abject as man destroy the very foundation of optimism? Freedom to do as our natures compelled us! Freedom to follow with accelerated feet the path that our fathers had worn! There was the rub.

It is obvious, however, that Geoffrey's pessimism is a temporary state, caused by the death of his parents, his financial indebtedness to Major Milward, and his hatred of bush farming. He is a melancholy, self-doubting young Hamlet of a man, but the optimism which is also a strong part of his nature eventually prevails. He frees himself by his actions.

In another section of the novel Geoffrey urges Lena Andersen to marry his young brother Robert, despite her own hesitation and reluctance to do so because her mother's adultery makes her feel unworthy of Robert. Geoffrey says: "Don't inquire too strenuously of the Fates, and happily they may forget us and pass by on the other side of the way." And thus when Geoffrey finally does decide to ignore the Fates and fight for his love for Eve, he finds that man indeed can have free choice in his actions. He frees himself from his self-doubts and achieves happiness at last, almost in the manner of an Existentialist hero.

Another character in *The Toll of the Bush*, the Englishman Wickener, is understandably fatalistic and pessimistic because his wife Laura has left him and he thinks that Geoffrey was the man responsible. "Nothing matters," he says. "Rattle it as you will, the game is in the box. That's fatalism." But then he too begins to fight against life and the rule of the Implacable Fates. He tells Sven Andersen to go back to his wife and act in his own welfare, asking, "Do you think Fate will wait your convenience?"

A change becomes apparent in Wickener's attitude to life as the novel progresses. Not only does he try in a perverse sort of way to help Sven Andersen; he also helps Lena Andersen, and pays Pine, the Maori, to keep on looking for Geoffrey and Eve when the lovers are lost in the bush. By helping others he recovers from his private feeling of doom and eventually redeems himself as a human being.

On the other hand, Sven Andersen, because of his alcoholism, is a prisoner of the Fates who cannot escape his doom despite Wickener's effort to help him. As Andersen goes off on his crazy journey to set fire to the Hokianga bush, Satchell interpolates a fatalistic sentence which might have come out of one of the tragedies of Aeschylus—or one of the novels of Thomas Hardy: "In the pauses of the wind a low mysterious shuddering made itself audible—a sound of awful majesty, one-toned, undying, afar, as it might be the roar of the great earth wheel through the gulf of space." But Satchell makes even this "shuddering" an ambiguous sound. It could well be, and probably is, the roar of surf on the bar at the river mouth, which has been mentioned frequently as being audible through the trees at that point in the county.

The persistence of the strain of fatalism in *The Toll of the Bush* comes out also in Mrs. Gird. She has learned to accept the fact that her paralyzed husband is slowly dying. She says to Lena: "The order of things is not changed in deference to human desire. In the end we have to make up our minds to the inevitable." The author's voice interpolates here: "The futility of hope is a tragic prospect to the young." Nevertheless, Satchell's attitude is finally optimistic; Lena soon sees that hope is not futile, for she marries Robert, and Geoffrey and Eve also find happiness together.

In *The Elixir of Life,* on the other hand, the fatalistic views expressed by Philip Westland arise from his illness, which he believes will soon kill him. He says to Isabel Vine: "It is time to choose our destiny. Probably in reality we have no choice. Fate like a skilful conjurer, merely forces the card, but we shall seem to have chosen." But his illness is completely cured by Vincent's elixir, while the love of Isabel buoys him up in his moments of defeatism. It is only in *The Greenstone Door* that Satchell's feelings of doom take undisputed control.

3 Revelation and Evolution

The romanticism of Satchell's fiction reflects his emotional bias toward the primitive, the innocent, and the natural part of life. He attacks what he considers to be the evils of modern civilization. Small businessmen like Arthur Roller and the Bromparts are shown to be immoral and unscrupulous, while a big businessman like Major Milward, who owns half the country and has a mortgage on the rest, is accepted because he really belongs to the past. He is one of the old pioneers who came before British rule was established. He is in his origin a romantic exile. He is a Purcell who made good—and is vaguely feudal. But there is one curious detail about both Milward and Purcell. They are religious doubters or agnostics—products of the scientific naturalism of the nineteenth century which tried to discredit Christianity—yet they also have a saving humanity in all their dealings with people.

Satchell's partial attack on Christianity is upon the sometimes hypocritical part it plays in community life—as in "A Martyr to Circumstantial Evidence." Thus Milward is no scientific materialist, and his anti-religious feeling is mainly a dislike of preachers in general. As he says to Geoffrey Hernshaw: "A parson is all very well to marry us and bury us and that sort of thing, but when he begins to distract our attention from the plain duty of sticking to our work he becomes a nuisance." He hates fanaticism, in short.

A few pages earlier Milward had remarked of the Reverend T. Fletcher:

"What makes religion such a cold, inhuman business when it's carried to excess? This Fletcher now, is there anything about him beyond what he *says?* If one wanted a fiver, would it be obtainable there sooner than elsewhere?"

Later it is stated that the Major "had the non-believer's prejudice against the Church as a body and objected to see his daughter pass over, as it were, to the arms of the enemy." Yet he agrees to her marriage to Fletcher, and sees that the wedding is a good one, properly carried out, because "to him the old forms and ceremonies were sacred things, not to be disregarded or slurred over." Is Major Milward, then, really anti-religious?

Such inconsistencies in the Major's thinking reveal a similar indecision in Satchell's mind, fluctuating in all his work between ironic scorn and agonized faith in Christianity. By his portrayal in depth of the thoughts of Eve Milward and of Fletcher himself—and by praising missionary accomplishments in *The Greenstone Door*—he shows how strongly his imagination was attracted to the belief in Christianity which his intelligence doubted and mocked in the words of Major Milward, Geoffrey Hernshaw, Cedric Tregarthen, and Purcell.

There is no doubt that he was interested very much in nineteenth century scientific naturalism, but he could not accept its materialism, which spurned the "beauty of life." Consequently in plotting *The Toll of the Bush* he works it so that Eve with her deep Christian faith should be repelled by Geoffrey's scientism. They debate the issue one afternoon in the office behind the store at Wairangi, where Eve, speaking first, takes the religious view, and exposes the religious side of Satchell.

"Do you think the story of Christ inadequate?"
"The moral teachings of Christ are one thing, and the Bible as an authentic account of the origin and history of the universe quite another."
"What is it you find so attractive in science? For mankind it seems to offer little, and for the individual nothing."
"But the road has gone only a little way into the darkness. It is paved with truths, and truths are hard to come by."
"Mr. Fletcher says that the *Origin of Species* does not disprove the Bible."
"The Church is wise, and I doubt if it would be possible to produce any argument which would disprove the Bible."
"I feel that revelation is quite as certain as evolution." [4]

Eve has the last word on this occasion, but when she eventually finds that Fletcher has tricked her into marrying him she asks herself: "Did God permit this? Then farewell to the dream that God existed." Later, when she runs away to hide in the wild bush country shortly after the wedding, and when Geoffrey finds her and comforts her, her Christian faith is restored, and she says: "I believe that God exists, and that He has not forgotten us. Was it a blind chance that led me without volition from that man to you—that fated we should meet at the one point on the road where no choice was left to us?" Here, God has superseded Fate.

Lena Andersen, who in many ways echoes Eve's thoughts, makes a similar remark to Geoffrey when she comments on her father's death in the bushfire: "What a terrible thing life is . . . and yet every now and then you seem to see the finger of God intervening, as though to prevent it from being worse. Is it as He would have it? Or has He also to wrestle with a Power nearly as great as Himself?" To which Geoffrey replies: "Men have thought so, Lena; they have founded their religion on that hypothesis."

Geoffrey uses one of Satchell's most striking images of the road to explain himself to Eve when he says that science is like

. . . the making of a road into the unknown. . . . the formed road men call Knowledge, and on it rests the foundation of the civilised world today. The extremities of the road are where the labourers in science are for ever probing the abyss and securing fresh foothold for the great journey; but its destination is that to which all religions alike turn their gaze—the origin of things, the fountain of Truth, the Absolute.

He anticipates the modern conclusions of thinkers like Fred Hoyle when he concedes that "science recognises that at some remote date she may reach a point where her tests will no longer meet with response, where the abyss will not yield to the plummet, and all the accumulated knowledge of the ages cannot carry her forward one single step." Geoffrey's final conclusion is that "each of us must believe according to his nature," and he retains his skepticism.

Passages like the above show that Satchell was closely in touch with avant garde trends as well as with the older romantic thinking of his day. Indeed, much of his unconventionalism and challenge to orthodoxy is near enough in kind to Olive Schreiner's type of high-voltage nonconformity, and to the general ideological potpourri in *The Story of an African Farm,* for it all to be seen conceivably as a part of the *Zeitgeist* from our point in history.

Satchell does not denounce Christianity; neither does he deny the value of science. What he rejects is any tendency to inhumanity in either of them; his attitude is the same as Major Milward's objection to Fletcher's "inhuman" religious zeal. His same concern for human values leads him to the irony of the poems "A Scientific Sing-Song" and "The Lay of the Scientific Man" with its sentence: "I cut with a knife the beauty of life." It is also the same concern that causes him to satirize the Christian missionary Mr. Hall in *The Greenstone Door* for failing to understand the Maoris as people; how could he hope to convert them if he did not take the trouble to learn their language and customs properly? Similarly the parson Mr. Milmouse in "A Matryr to Circumstantial Evidence" is condemned for bringing the wharf man Bagstock to his death because of an entirely false assumption that he was guilty of theft.

4   Titanic Nature

In Satchell's fiction man is generally measured against nature. If nature is strong, solid, and enduring, then man is pitiable by contrast. This is most apparent to Sven Andersen, who cannot cope with life in the bush. He gives way to bouts of drunkenness, and sees "on one side the titanic forces of nature, inexorable, eternal; on the other man, frail of body, the creature of an hour, "matching himself against them." But Sven Andersen is a failure, despite his heroic final act of rescuing his children from Beckwith's burning house.

The most important characters in Satchell's fiction are equal to the forces of nature and harness them: thus Major Milward and Purcell are heroic pioneers who tame the wilderness to their desire and create an ideal rural community. Hugh Clifford gives up an inheritance to live close to nature on the gumfield, and in doing so finds the love of a woman and redemption as a man.

Cedric Tregarthen refuses a chance to become an English lord
to stay with the Maoris in the bush. Geoffrey Hernshaw finds
success in his love for Eve when they are lost in the bush. The
closer a man gets to nature, it would appear, the greater his
worth proves to be and the greater his success in life's struggles.
Those who fail are the "lost" whose past acts have already condemned them to death in the wilderness.

Women are the same. Meri, the Maori girl in "After His
Kind," is preferred by Merton to the frivolous, sociable Mildred
McGregor. Esther and Eve love the bush and admire the Maoris
who, longtime inhabitants of the bush, "have a hatred of the
meanness and paltriness that is associated with so much of our
civilised system of money-making," and have more "human
merit" than small businessmen like Arthur Roller with his delu-
sive pretensions of superiority based merely on the fact that he
is a white man. Eve's religious impulse leads inevitably to a kind
of pantheism which is Wordsworthian in its romanticism; to her
the bush is a "temple of life." Esther has a similar reaction; in
the kauri forest she feels she is "riding through a cathedral."
Her cousin Wilfred also sees the forest as "the abode of the
gods." And when Eve and Geoffrey stand beneath a giant kauri
tree, Satchell interpolates his own authorial comment (they are
lost in the bush):

> The pair stood still, forgetful of self, in that mute reverence which the
> mighty works of Nature must for ever arouse in the heart of man. . . .
> So for awhile they stood in all but perfect understanding. And over
> them the kauri spread his leafy screen. Rooted in the centuries, he
> had watched through a thousand generations of man the fleeting
> shadows on the forest floor. And still they came and went.[5]

There is here an obvious if unstated parallel with Adam and
Eve in the Garden of Eden before the Fall which came with
Knowledge—equated in Satchell's imagination with the road into
the wilderness.

For Eve, nature also means a refuge from treachery and a
release from pain. As she gallops off on horseback into the bush
after finding that Fletcher has tricked her into marriage, she
thinks: "Oh, to be away beyond the reach of curious eyes and
interrogating voices, alone with the sweet silences of Nature!"

The healing properties of nature are again strikingly illustrated by Sven Andersen's brief rehabilitation when he works as a bushman on the new road and is temporarily "purified and strengthened" by his work as a bush-faller.

Geoffrey's comment, previously quoted—"Woe to the man who, in this new land, struggling with the giant forces of nature, should stand to count the cost or ask himself what he desired"—shows the importance to man of the struggle with titanic nature, and the need for victory. Then Andersen's brief period of real work as a bushman makes clear that the struggle itself brings out the best qualities in man, makes him "strong and resolute" by matching him against something that is vast and eternal, so that even in defeat he becomes supremely a man.

Nature's rules, rather than the "puny conventions" of society, are also the best guide to moral behavior, at least in the early books, for it must be remembered that in *The Greenstone Door*, Purcell is destroyed by society for obeying natural law. But Purcell's sin, his hubris, is pride—he is too proud to be a good citizen, and stands aloof even from the Maori community which he dominates. In the early novels a different mood prevails. Mrs. Andersen finds real happiness with Beckwith—a radiance that is attributed to "the strong hand of Nature, which, regardless of the puny conventions of mankind and of the suffering of the individual, fixes forever her summoning eye on the things not of today but of tomorrow." Can one detect here a note of irony, since it is this act of Mrs. Andersen's which causes Sven Andersen to start the bushfire which destroys the forest and causes his own death?

In *The Land of the Lost* Hugh Clifford also, and logically, declares in favor of natural rather than conventional behavior during his courtship of Esther: "I suppose convention is a sort of mental clothing," he says; "it has its fashions, like our coats, and is continually on the change, but we always wear it in some form or other. It is only under the influence of strong emotions that we throw it aside and become completely natural." Although Esther laughs off his remark at the time, her later acts show that she agrees that behavior should be "completely natural" as far as possible.

Another piece of individual suffering which results from Mrs. Andersen's desertion of her husband is its effect on her daughter

Lena. Lena's agony is pitiful to observe. It drives her into a suicidal mood from which only Robert's strength and gentleness rescue her. Mrs. Gird helps Lena by telling her that it is impossible for anyone to do always what is perfectly right, later emphasizing her belief in natural behavior and her belief in "true love" in a further talk with Lena.

"I am on the side of true love every time, and not blindly, but with all the light God has given me. When I see it pure and unselfish, then I know that I am in the presence of a thing that is beautiful and holy, and I would array myself on its side though all the conventions of the world were leagued in opposition."

But she too has good cause to speak, because her husband's paralysis mocks her married life. Similarly Alan Vincent in *The Elixir of Life* challenges the worth of a loveless marriage.

From all the above it appears that to Satchell's way of thinking the best kind of love is that which is "natural" or unconventional, or "true" in the sense of the troubadours that true love is adulterous love. In other words, romantic love is his ideal. But he deals in his novels with many varieties of love.

5 *Varieties of Love*

The virtuous young heroes of a Satchell novel always marry into a good family: in this way their position as future leaders of the community is made certain. But they are such good clean men that their love affairs are idealized almost beyond human interest. It is the other varieties of love in Satchell's fiction which provide his most interesting motive forces. From the love of Merton for his Maori girl Meri to Purcell's love for the slave girl Roma, any human affection is shown to be of great value for those living a life of hardship: not only romantic love between a man and a woman, but the father-son love between Purcell and Cedric or between Jessamine Olive and Bart, the cousinly love between Wilfred and Esther Hamilton, the father-daughter love between Dr. Hamilton and Esther and between Major Milward and Eve, the brotherly friendship between Cedric and Rangiora, or Cedric's affection for his foster-sister Puhi-Huia. Each of these strong relationships has its influence on the course of events. Finally, not least important among these motivating forces is the Christianity which the missionaries in *The Greenstone Door* bring to the Maori tribes and which is, somewhat ironically, called "that message of love" which will release them from the savage world of darkness and bring them a life of peace and happiness.

Love is the magical feeling which transforms character and heals the wounds caused by a hostile environment or unfortunate events. Thus it is Hugh Clifford's compensation for his period of exile on the gumfield that he meets Esther Hamilton. Dr. Hamilton's love for Esther causes him finally to change his attitude toward the gumdigger from hostility to friendship. Jessamine Olive's affection for Bart causes him to watch over the alcoholic and protect him from the gumfield ruffians, and Jess's visit to the bush pub to take Bart away from a drunken party there causes the long, violent sequence which forms the climax of *The Land of the Lost.*

At the beginning of *The Toll of the Bush,* Geoffrey Hernshaw feels that he would have returned to England but for his love for Eve Milward, because for him as for most men "the place where love dwells is the only spot more desirable than that where we were born and bred." Love is the driving force behind Sven Andersen's brief recovery of his manhood during his three months' spell as a bushman on the new road, as a result of which he hopes to win back his wife's affection: "as the American steel axe circled and fell, he conjured up the scenes of that second wooing . . . and with respect would come love." His discovery that he has lost her love irretrievably when she goes to live with Beckwith causes him to start the great Hokianga bushfire which provides the novel's violent climax.

Andersen's death, while rescuing from the fire the children whom he loves, causes Geoffrey to say: "No man could meet a more honourable end than to die a great death in the cause of humanity." But later on Geoffrey himself is reproached by Eve for not forcing his love on her more vigorously against Fletcher's rivalry. "You should have held me by force,—you should have compelled me to listen—to believe. If you had killed me for my obstinacy I should have died worshipping you. . . . I loved you—I loved only you. Every hour which brought me nearer to him was an agony—yet you stood by." Satchell condemns Geoffrey for not following his desire and his dream—for not loving strongly and deeply enough, until it is almost too late.

Philip Westland in *The Elixir of Life* is another who risks his life in the name of humanity when he lets Dr. Alan Vincent test the serum on him. Vincent tells him that part of the cure for his medical condition is love: "I say love is necessary to you— the love of a woman, a wife." And when Vincent asks Grace Severne to be his adulterous mistress, she decides that "love was worth the price to be paid for it" even if the price "goes on for ever."

The many varieties of love used in the narrative of *The Greenstone Door*, and the destruction of most of them in the chaos of the Maori Wars, fill this last novel with all its great intensity of feeling. Purcell's decision to give military advice to the Maoris, though firing no actual shots against the British troops, is made purely on the grounds of love, as he explains his action in a letter to Cedric.

Though we avoided speech I think you have guessed, or even known, for two or three years past that a position of neutrality could never be mine. My wife is a native woman; my child is the daughter of a native woman. Nature knows no stronger bond than that which binds us to wife and child. . . . From the point of view of the patriot I am doubtless a monster, but considered as merely a human being it may be that I have my redeeming points . . . for thirty years these have been my people, and for thirty years their country has been my home . . . I should be a sorry knave if I deserted my friends in their need, or failed to strike a blow in defence of those I love.[6]

A more dramatic instance of the love motive in the plot of *The Greenstone Door* occurs in Chapter VIII, titled "The Triumph of Love—and of Darkness." Cedric, at this stage of the story a small boy, goes in company with Purcell and the missionary Mr. Hall and a band of young Maoris from Matakiki, to visit the fortress called Pahuata, hilltop home of the old chief. On his journey along the bush track, Cedric sees the youths of their "war party" kill the imaginary "flying fish" which crosses in front of their "war canoe," not knowing that he will soon himself become the metaphorical flying fish (which

was sacrificed before a battle to the gods of war) when Huata
tries to kill him as a token of his hostility to the invading white
man.

Huata orders Cedric to be killed primarily in order to revenge
himself on Purcell for bringing another white man to his fort, in
violation of their agreement, and to show his contempt for the
missionary's message of love. Cedric runs wildly around the flat,
open space inside the palisades, avoiding by extraordinary speed
and agility the clubs of the warriors sent to kill him, until a
sudden silence causes him to look up.

In the centre of the guard, holding them arrested at a distance of a
few yards by the threatening of his upraised hand, stood my father.
In his right hand was a heavy pistol, and—his temple against its
muzzle—stood Rangiora, clothed in his cloak of dog-skin, his head
erect, his eyes calm and steadfast. No hand of violence rested upon
him. He stood there, as my heart plainly told me, in the cause of a
friendship that passed the love of woman, offering his love for mine
. . . white or brown or black, what mattered it to me! I knew then,
as I know today, that no brighter spirit ever inhabited a tabernacle
of human flesh.[7]

Rangiora had actually put the pistol in Purcell's hand in order
to defy his own father, Huata. He had done this in accordance
with the *tatau pounamu* or greenstone door compact (the inter-
racial "bond of love" previously described) that the two boys
had made after Rangiora had saved Cedric's life in the river.
The incident is handled differently in a manuscript version of
the novel where Rangiora throws himself at Cedric and knocks
him down and shields him with his own body from the warriors' clubs. But the dramatic effect is the same.

The bond of love also links Cedric to his foster father and
foster-sister. Purcell sends Cedric to Auckland to complete his
education, and places a large sum of money at his disposal,
because "I love you; that is the why and wherefore." Cedric, as
if in response to this claim, when he learns his true identity in
Auckland and is asked by Lady Wylde to return to England to
live with Lord Tregarthen his grandfather, says that he cannot
leave his foster-father and Puhi-Huia. "Nothing could recompense them. You see . . . they love me." He also feels that even

if the elopement of his dead father and mother was "dishon-
ourable on high moral counts, it stood absolved in the courts
of Love."

Finally when Cedric has lost everything—has seen Purcell,
Rangiora, and Puhi-Huia killed in the war—he is restored to
health after the shock had sent him temporarily insane, by the
affection of Helenora, who goes off into the bush where he is
hiding in a cave to find him and nurse him. But again it is nature, the wilderness, which performs the first part of the treatment. It is worth noting in this passage how Cedric too in his
moment of crisis becomes the "solitary wanderer" so typical of
Satchell's romanticism, as Purcell was before him.

I have often wondered if it was some blessed instinct that urged me
thus into the wilds, far from the haunts and taunts of men; that made
of me a solitary wanderer, braving all weathers, careless of rain and
storm, of the damp earth that formed my couch, sleeping with the
sun and rising with it, till the health of a wild animal pervaded my
body and the cloud lifted and passed away from my brain.[8]

When romantic love combines with nature to effect the cure,
the reunion of Cedric and Helenora takes place in a cave where
he sleeps with a small cooking fire burning at its entrance.
"Giddy and half blind, I groped my way to the cave and sank
into my couch of fern fronds." There Helenora comforts him,
until "in God's good time and at the call of Love I awoke, and
my madness had passed and left no vestige in memory."

This cave episode resembles the incident near the end of *The
Toll of the Bush*, where Geoffrey and Eve lie in each other's
arms in their fern shelter in the middle of the Waipoua kauri
forest, after they have been lost in the bush for several days
and nights. The same image of a cave occurs in *The Land of the
Lost*, in the tent on the gumfield. Here, Hugh Clifford and
Esther fall in love while Esther lies on a couch of fern and
watches the campfire at the entrance.

The little cave at the end of *The Greenstone Door*, in which
Cedric and Helenora are reunited, is also suggestively related to
death. "A golden beam slanted to the entrance of my retreat,
and down it—as an angel of heaven might come to the gateway
of death—came Helenora." The big limestone cave at the be-

ginning of the book was the secret center of the childhood love of Puhi-Huia and Rangiora. Here another association of cave, love and death is plain, and here the meaning is pessimistic in inter-racial terms: the menacing limestone curtain warned of their deaths in the figures of the weeping woman and the gourd, and the shapeless thing at her feet.

In *The Land of the Lost,* however, where Esther is Hugh's rescuing angel on the gumfield, their tent is the place where Brice tries to shoot her. The attempt fails. Similarly in *The Toll of the Bush,* the fern shelter where Geoffrey and Eve find their love for each other in the bush, was also expected to be their death-bed, since they are dying of starvation and have given up all hope of rescue. These parallels serve to show how the customary linking of love and death in romantic literature has taken place in Satchell's imagination through a fusion of various cave images.

Another aspect of his romanticism can be seen in the fact that love in his fiction can only flourish in a natural setting. In the city, love fails to grow. For instance the unproductive love affair between Cedric and Sarah Brompart in Auckland is a city love. The love between Merton and Mildred McGregor in Auckland disintegrates in the dream sequence of the story "After His Kind." Even the false love between Eve Milward and Fletcher falters when they go to Auckland.

By contrast the love of Esther Hamilton and Hugh Clifford begins in the wilderness of the gumfield. Their subsequent court-ship occurs outdoors in the luxuriant garden and bush-house (a kind of summer-house) of Dr. Hamilton's colonial home. Eve Milward and Geoffrey Hernshaw cannot admit their love for each other at Wairangi homestead, the social center of *The Toll of the Bush,* but are united after they become lost in the Fifty-Mile Bush, cut off from other people. Robert and Lena Andersen carry on their courtship in the bush. Even the loves of Alan Vincent and Grace Severne, of Philip Westland and Isabel Vine, come to fruition on the island, not on the ship. Purcell finds love among the Maoris after he has renounced civilization.

Admittedly Cedric and Helenora fall in love in Auckland, but their courtship scenes occur in the gardens of Government House. Whenever Cedric meets her indoors, his love attempts are frustrated. Also, love at Government House is in a sense a false love, since we learn subsequently that Helenora at this time does not really love Cedric but is leading him on cold-heartedly in order to revenge the hurt done to her mother by his father long ago in England. It is only when Helenora comes down into the bush country of the Waipa Valley, in search of Cedric after the war is over, that their love becomes real.

One final fusion takes place in Satchell's imagination: the linking of love and law, which ties up the loose ends of his thinking about such matters as civilization and the wilderness, science and religion, love and death, or conventional and natural behavior. The passage where the connection is made most vital occurs in *The Toll of the Bush,* but the idea of law as a supreme force is constant in all the fiction, even where it is not associated with love.

Civilization must prevail. That is Satchell's conclusion and the moral message of his novels, if a message is needed. All his heroes are educated men, lovers of good books. Although he is emotionally in sympathy with his outcasts and "lost" characters, including the Maoris, he realizes man's need for law and order through the "formed road" of science and knowledge.

Civilization must prevail, in the mind of Geoffrey Hernshaw, even if he sometimes doubts that it is worth the cost in the loss of men's lives and the destruction of natural beauty. It must prevail, in the mind of Cedric Tregarthen, even if it works disastrous effects on the ancient Maori culture. Sir George Grey prevails over Purcell because, though both are equal in their love of learning, Grey is on the side of law and civilization and Purcell is an outsider and finally an outlaw. The other early pioneers who are admired by Cedric and Geoffrey are those who tame the wilderness and build their new cities in the new land. Philip Westland is cured of his sickness because the rebellious cells in his body have been "reinspired with that spirit of order without which health is impossible." In much the same way, Purcell and his warring Maoris, as the rebellious unit in society, must perish if they do not submit to law and order. Evil-doers like Upmore and Brice are also destroyed by society for revolting against the codes of civilization. Only in the cause of a great romantic love may the conventions of society be violated, and even then society will exact its price, which may go on "for ever." Such a love can lead, as it does with Purcell, to the supreme price of death, since it is his wife Roma who accidentally makes his execution certain.

But love and law are found by Geoffrey and Eve in *The Toll of the Bush* to be really the same, merely the opposite sides of one coin. She asks him, in one of their discussions on the merits of science versus religion:

> "Is there nothing that comes to you . . . out of the great Unknown?"
> "Yes," he said steadily. "Law, unchanging, adequate, unconfused."
> "And to me—Love." [9]

Geoffrey then suggests that this may be "the reverse of the coin," and a basis for understanding between them: "Love that is bound by law, and law that is inspired by love." Although this smacks of word-spinning, it is still in essence the final expression of Satchell's thought on the problems of human existence, with special implications for the multiracial civilization of the new world which he saw slowly coming to the South Pacific.

It was E.H. McCormick in his *Letters and Art in New Zealand* (1940) and *New Zealand Literature: A Survey* (1959) who saw the historical importance of Satchell as the last of the colonial novelists writing about exiled British lords and remittance men of the nineteenth century—a view which Joan Stevens largely agrees with in *The New Zealand Novel 1860-1965* (1966). But Dr. McCormick also saw the importance of Satchell's work as a model for future novelists, notably Jane Mander, who particularly in *The Story of a New Zealand River* (1920) and *Allen Adair* (1925) also writes of life in the North Auckland gumfields and bush settlements, but with a more feminist outlook.

Today a younger generation of critics, such as Les Cleveland and the poet Louis Johnson, see Satchell also as an apparent inspiration to Frank Sargeson, who was born in 1903, and as the "grandfather" (to use Johnson's word) of many younger novelists—a forerunner with the themes of social alienation and the search for identity which are characteristic of the work of Janet Frame, Ian Cross, Maurice Duggan, Maurice Gee, and Maurice Shadbolt—I have referred to my own debt to Satchell. Errol Brathwaite's Maori Wars trilogy, which began with *The Flying Fish* (1964) and *The Needle's Eye* (1965), is obviously indebted to *The Greenstone Door* in a general way, though Brathwaite's attitude to the Maoris' role in the conflict is very different from Satchell's. More particularly, Satchell's view of brown New Zealand is reflected in the handling of Maori characters in the contemporary novels of Sylvia Ashton-Warner, Charles Frances, Bill Pearson, O.E. Middleton, Noel Hilliard, and others. The movement is carried to a further degree of completely casual, if incidental, acceptance of Maori characters in a novel like Jean Watson's *Stand in the Rain* (1965) or the tales of E.H. Audley, where there is a form of neo-romanticism which looks back to the idealized Maoris and unfortunate social outcasts in Satchell's fiction.

In his last three novels Satchell tries to speak for all mankind, out of an ongoing concern with man's basic condition. *The Greenstone Door* in particular glows with a fierce idealism. "Does your humanity still see a way of escape?" Sir George Grey asks Cedric when war appears to be inevitable. Mankind's general needs are the only worthwhile measuring rod for conduct. Thus Purcell's death is more than just a rebuke aimed at poor race relations in New Zealand's early days, or a condemnation of the pettiness and hypocrisy of her early society, once the great days of the explorers and whalers and traders had passed. Purcell asks in fact to be judged simply as a man. That is why, in his defiant speech at the court martial, he renounces his British citizenship. "I deny that I am a British subject. I was in this country before—if ever—it became a possession of the Queen's." As with all of Satchell's tragic characters, the dignity of the man persists through and in spite of defeat.

Satchell decided, in his portraits of a pioneer society, to show the high price of civilization—in the waste of noble lives, in the loss of natural beauty, and in the destruction of so much ancient Maori culture. His novels also show the chaos into which so many human relationships can fall—because of the violence in the lives of his early New Zealand settlers and the urgency of their needs. But he had to believe that such a toll was worth paying, because civilization is man's path to the stars, because chaos and destruction eventually lead to a new order.

It is this broad concern for man's fate which is the key to Satchell's universal appeal. His use of the English language to present his novels was eloquent and often splendidly successful, despite his lapses. His romanticism and his pessimism were well adapted to his task; they helped give him an insight into the beauties and defects of all human existence. In his vision of life on the South Pacific frontier of nineteenth century civilization, the dark beauty of his imaginative conceptions and the moral truth of the spiritual and intellectual order he created, are unique in world literature.

Notes and References

CHAPTER ONE

1. All quotations from Satchell's letters are from the Satchell Papers held by the Alexander Turnbull Library in Wellington, New Zealand.
2. From *His Island Home; and Away in the Far North* (Wellington, 1879).
3. *New Zealand Graphic,* October 19, and November 23, 1895.
4. From the private collection of Satchell material held by George Satchell.
5. Satchell Papers.
6. Satchell Papers.

CHAPTER TWO

1. *Will o' the Wisp* (London, 1883), p. 25.
2. *N.Z. Graphic,* September 15, 1894.
3. *Ibid.,* January 11, 1896.
4. *The Red Funnel,* July 1, 1906.
5. *N.Z. Herald,* July 17, 1915.

CHAPTER THREE

1. *The Land of the Lost* (London, 1902), pp. 70-1.
2. *Ibid.,* pp. 55, 149.
3. *The Toll of the Bush* (London, 1905), p. 45.
4. *Ibid.,* p. 275.
5. *Ibid.,* pp. 148, 189.
6. *Ibid.,* p. 146.
7. *Ibid.,* p. 357.
8. *Ibid.,* p. 236.
9. *Ibid.,* pp. 255-6.
10. *Ibid.,* p. 385.
11. *Ibid.,* p. 402.

Chapter Four

1. *The Elixir of Life* (London, 1907), p. 213.
2. *Ibid.,* p. 29.
3. *Ibid.,* p. 98.
4. *Ibid.,* p. 165.
5. *Ibid.,* p. 216.
6. *Ibid.,* pp. 295-6.

Chapter Five

1. *The Greenstone Door* (London & New York, 1914), p. 47.
2. *Ibid.,* p. 193.
3. *Ibid.,* pp. 195-6.
4. *Ibid.,* p. 387.
5. *Ibid.,* p. 2.
6. *Ibid.,* p. 71.
7. From the manuscript in the Auckland Public Library.
8. *The Greenstone Door,* p. 44.
9. *Ibid.,* pp. 155-6.
10. *Ibid.,* p. 244.
11. *Ibid.,* pp. 369-70.
12. *Ibid.,* p. 380.
13. *Ibid.,* p. 92.
14. *Ibid.,* pp. 110-11.

Chapter Six

1. *The Greenstone Door,* pp. 49-50.
2. *The Land of the Lost,* p. 308.
3. *The Elixir of Life,* pp. 4-5.
4. *The Toll of the Bush,* p. 80.
5. *Ibid.,* pp. 381-2.
6. *The Greenstone Door,* pp. 357-8.
7. *Ibid.,* p. 105.
8. *Ibid.,* p. 392.
9. *The Toll of the Bush,* p. 149.

Selected Bibliography

PRIMARY SOURCES

(Works by William Satchell, in chronological order.)

Bedlam Ballads and Straitwaistcoat Stories. London: W. Satchell and Co., 1883.

Will o' the Wisp and Other Tales in Prose and Verse. London: W. Satchell and Co., 1883.

"The Great Unemployed Scheme," *The New Zealand Graphic,* June 16, 1894.

"A Football Match," *N.Z. Graphic,* July 7, 1894.

"Why I Came to New Zealand," *N.Z. Graphic,* August 25, 1894.

"Emotions of an Emigrant," *N.Z. Graphic,* September 15, 1894.

"Things in Heaven and Earth," *N.Z. Graphic,* October 20, 1894.

"From a Northern Gumfield," *N.Z. Graphic,* November 3, 1894.

"The Man Who Went North," *N.Z. Graphic,* September 7, 1895.

"An Author's Model," *N.Z. Graphic,* November 16, 1895.

"The Yellow Dwarf," *N.Z. Graphic,* November 23, 1895.

"A Martyr to Circumstantial Evidence," *N.Z. Graphic,* January 11, 1896.

Patriotic and Other Poems. Auckland: The Brett Printing and Publishing Co., 1900.

The Maorilander, Numbers 1-7. Published by William Satchell at the office of the Paper, Exchange Lane, Auckland, February 8–March 22, 1901. (Contains "The Stone Stable Mystery," "The Stiff 'Un," "Laughing War Off the Face of the Earth," "Mr. Pilcher's Garden," "Herr Lieber's Melons," "The Deserters," "The Babes in the Bush," "Te Kotira Ma," "Wilkes' Sanatorium.").

The Land of the Lost. London: Methuen and Co., 1902; Christchurch: Whitcombe and Tombs, 1938.

"The Divided Note," *N.Z. Graphic,* January 2, 1904.

"The Stone Stable Mystery," *N.Z. Graphic,* April 23–May 14, 1904.

The Toll of the Bush. London: Macmillan and Co., 1905.

"After His Kind," *The Red Funnel,* July 1, 1906.

The Elixir of Life. London: Chapman and Hall, 1907.

The Greenstone Door. London: Sidgwick and Jackson, 1914; New York: the Macmillan Co., 1914; Christchurch: Whitcombe and Tombs, 1935.

"God and the War," *N.Z. Herald*, May 15, 1915.
"Ourselves and the War," *N.Z. Herald*, June 5, 1915.
"The Truth About the War," *N.Z. Herald*, June 19, 1915.
"Afterwards," *N.Z. Herald*, July 3, 1915.
"The Racial Delusion," *N.Z. Herald*, July 17, 1915.
"Nothing to Fight For," *N.Z. Herald*, July 24, 1915.
"Management v. Government," *N.Z. Herald*, August 7, 1915.
"War's Place in Nature," *N.Z. Herald*, September 4, 1915.
"The Great Adventure," *N.Z. Herald*, October 2, 1915.
"The Dream City," *N.Z. Herald*, October 9, 1915.
"The Man of Destiny," *N.Z. Herald*, October 23, 1915.
"Genius for Victory," *N.Z. Herald*, November 6, 1915.
"For Food or For Honours," *N.Z. Herald*, August 12, 1916.
"Trees and Spires," *N.Z. Herald*, September 2, 1916.
"The World's Danger," *N.Z. Herald*, September 16, 1916.
"The Child and the State," *N.Z. Herald*, September 23, 1916.
"Winning the War," *N.Z. Herald*, March 30, 1918.
"Equality," *N.Z. Herald*, May 4, 1918.

The James B. Pinker Papers, which contain some material relevant to Satchell, are in the Rare Books Room at Northwestern University, Evanston, Illinois. The Satchell Papers are in the Alexander Turnbull Library, Wellington, New Zealand. The manuscript of *The Greenstone Door* is in the Auckland Public Library.

SECONDARY SOURCES

FEA, ALLAN. *Recollections of Sixty Years*. London: The Richards Press, 1927. Contains some personal reminiscences. Minor.

GRIES, JOAN C. *An Outline of Prose Fiction in New Zealand*. (Unpublished thesis, Auckland University College, 1951). Part Three (2) is good, negative criticism.

McCORMICK, E. H. *Letters and Art in New Zealand*. Wellington: Department of Internal Affairs, 1940. Chapter Six includes excellent criticism.

———. *New Zealand Literature: A Survey*. London: The Oxford University Press, 1959. Revises earlier assessment.

PEARSON, W. H. "Attitudes to the Maori in Some Pakeha Fiction," *Polynesian Society Journal*, LXVII, No. 3 (September, 1958), 211-238. Good background reference.

SMITH, E. M. *A History of New Zealand Fiction*. Dunedin: A. H. & A. W. Reed, 1939. Contains some brief comments.

STEVENS, JOAN. *The New Zealand Novel 1860-1965*. Wellington: A. H. & A. W. Reed, 1966. Includes passages of concise criticism.

WALL, NANCY. *Representation of the Maori in Pakeha Fiction.* (Unpublished thesis, University of Otago, 1961). Some good appreciation.
WILSON, PHILLIP. *The Maorilander: A Study of William Satchell.* Christchurch: Whitcombe and Tombs, 1961. Full critical analysis.

Index

Date Due

DEMCO NO. 25-370
